# Quick & Easy
# Vegetarian Pasta

*p*

# Contents

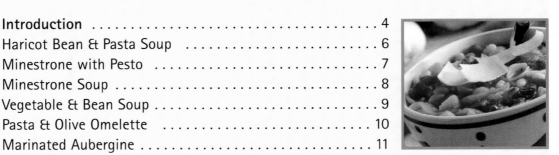

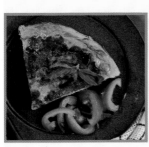

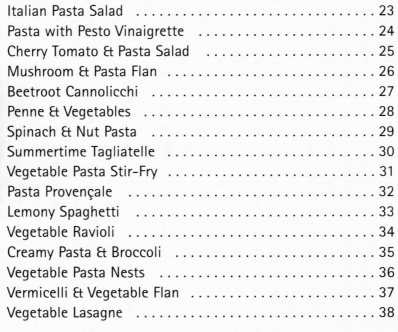

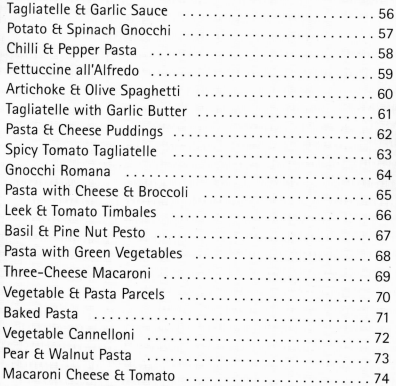

# Introduction

**Pasta is one of the most versatile and easy foods to cook and lends itself perfectly to a vegetarian diet. It can be combined with a variety of ingredients to create differently flavoured and textured dishes which both vegetarians and those who eat meat will adore. Vegetarian Pasta has collected together some of the most traditional Italian recipes with innovative new dishes which cater for a variety of tastes. The superb combination of vegetables, herbs and pasta means that the dishes are not only colourful but nutritious too.**

## Healthy Vegetarian

In eating vegetarian pasta dishes, you not only benefit from the healthy ingredients used in Mediterranean

cuisine, such as olive oil, garlic and red wine, but also from the nutritional advantages and low-fat content of the vegetarian gastronomy. These two culinary influences create flavoursome and balanced dishes that provide plenty of fibre, carbohydrates, vitamins and minerals. Contrary to common belief, pasta is not a fattening food but is predominantly made up of complex carbohydrates, which slowly release vital energy supplies into our blood streams. On its own, pasta is an excellent source of protein, which comes from its main ingredient, durum wheat. The dark flecks which are visible in dried pasta are wheatgerm that has not been removed but ground up in the flour. This will add to the relatively high protein content (around 70%). However, large amounts of flecks can indicate excess bran, which makes the pasta rough and harsh. When eaten with a rich vegetable sauce and a slice of wholewheat bread, most of the food groups are represented in this diet.

Many Italian sauces are made from fresh vegetables and fruit, which contain calcium, iron and phosphorous. Fruit and vegetables are essential for healthy living as they are great sources of vitamins. Vitamin A is found

in green, yellow and orange vegetables, and particularly in carrots. Leafy vegetables are an excellent source of vitamin E. Vitamin C is present in many 'fruit vegetables', such as peppers and tomatoes – favourites of the Italian diet – and may also be found in the roots and leaves of others. In order to supplement the lack of protein usually provided by meat, pulses, which are naturally high in this essential nutrient, can also be eaten.

## Pasta

There are hundreds of different types of pasta of varying shapes, colours and sizes, and new pasta is being made all the time. Basic pasta is made from durum wheat flour and water (*pasta* means 'dough' or 'paste' in Italian), while *pasta all'uova* is enriched with eggs. Other ingredients are added, such as spinach and squid ink, to produce different colours and flavours.

It is worth buying fresh pasta, called *maccheroni* in Italy, from a good delicatessen. Otherwise, fresh unfilled pasta is not really any better than the dried variety. There are no hard and fast rules about which pasta should be served with which sauce. As a guide, long, thin types of pasta, such as fettuccine, tagliatelle, spaghetti and taglioni, are best for delicate, olive-oil-based and seafood sauces. Short, fat pasta shapes, such as lumache, conchiglie and penne, or curly shapes such as farfalle and fusilli, are best for heavier sauces, as they

trap pieces of vegetables from the sauce and stop them from sinking to the bottom of the dish. Tiny pasta shapes, such as stellete, pepe bucato and risi, are used for soups. However, the names of pasta can change depending on the region of Italy you are in and on manufacturers, so look carefully at the size and shape before purchasing. Certain suffixes denote a particular size of pasta: -etti or -ette means small, as in spaghetti and farfallette (little strings and little butterflies); -ini or -ine means very small as in sedanini and lumachine (tiny celery and tiny snails); and -oni and -one mean large as in farfalloni and lumacone (large butterflies and large snails).

## Basic Pasta Dough
If you wish to make your own pasta for the dishes in this book, follow this simple recipe.
**Ingredients**
450 g/1 lb/4 cups durum wheat flour
4 eggs, lightly beaten
1 tbsp olive oil
salt
1. Lightly flour a work surface (counter). Sift the flour with a pinch of salt into a mound. Make a well in the centre and add the eggs and olive oil.
2. Using a fork or your fingertips, gradually work the mixture until the ingredients are combined. Knead vigorously for 10–15 minutes.
3. Set the dough aside to rest for 25 minutes, before rolling it out as thinly and evenly as possible.

## Cooking Dried Pasta the Classic Way
The classic way to cook 500 g (1 lb) of dried spaghetti is in 10 pints (6 litres) of salted boiling water. It should be occasionally stirred with a fork to ensure that the pieces do not stick together. Doing this also means that you need not add oil to the water, which raises the calorie content of the dish and stops the sauce from sticking to the spaghetti. The length of cooking time depends on the thickness of the pasta, how dry it is and the humidity, so follow the guidelines on the packet. However, before the cooking time is up test one piece of pasta:

it should be firm to the bite. After draining the pasta, do not rinse but return it to a warm pan and do not let it dry out, otherwise the pieces will stick together. Add the sauce and serve in warm, shallow soup-plates.

## Cooking Vegetarian for the First Time
For those who have decided to convert to vegetarianism and are cooking meat-free food for the first time, there are several ingredients that should be avoided. In particular, avoid gelatine, a protein used to thicken foods. It is used in many puddings, but it is made from collagen, so a vegetarian substitute should be used instead. When buying pre-packaged ingredients, in particular sweet foods such as biscuits, always check the ingredients to see if animal fats have been used. You should also be aware that some condiments, such as Worcestershire Sauce, which is made using anchovies, may contain animal products.

## The Cheese Issue
Although some cheeses are made with vegetarian ingredients, many contain animal derivatives: strict vegetarians should buy those that have been certified by the Vegetarian Society and have a green 'V' on the label. Vegetarian cheeses are made with rennet of non-animal origin, using microbial or fungal enzymes. Italian recipes frequently contain cheese, so you may want to make sure that you have a suitable vegetarian variety before you start cooking. In general, most soft cheeses are suitable for vegetarians and there are plenty of alternatives or vegetarian versions of traditional cheeses. As a guide, Parmesan is generally non-vegetarian but there is an Italian Parmesan called Grano Padano which usually is vegetarian. Vegetarian feta, Cheddar, Cheshire, red Leicester, dolcelatte and goats' cheeses can be bought in larger supermarkets or from specialist health food and vegetarian shops.

| | KEY |
|---|---|
|  | Simplicity level 1 – 3 (1 easiest, 3 slightly harder) |
|  | Preparation time |
|  | Cooking time |

# Haricot Bean & Pasta Soup

This soup makes an excellent winter lunch served with warm crusty bread and a slice of cheese.

## NUTRITIONAL INFORMATION

| | | | |
|---|---|---|---|
| Calories | 584 | Sugars | 13g |
| Protein | 22g | Fat | 29g |
| Carbohydrate | 63g | Saturates | 5g |

3¼ HRS          1¼ HRS

### SERVES 4

## INGREDIENTS

250 g/9 oz/1⅓ cups haricot (navy) beans, soaked for 3 hours in cold water and drained

4 tbsp olive oil

2 large onions, sliced

3 garlic cloves, chopped

425 g/14 oz can chopped tomatoes

1 tsp dried oregano

1 tsp tomato purée (paste)

850 ml/1½ pints/3½ cups water

90 g/3½ oz/¾ cup dried fusilli or conchigliette

115 g/4 oz sun-dried tomatoes, drained and thinly sliced

1 tbsp chopped fresh coriander (cilantro) or flat leaf parsley

salt and pepper

2 tbsp Parmesan cheese shavings, to serve

1 Put the haricot (navy) beans in a large pan. Cover with cold water and bring to the boil. Boil vigorously for 15 minutes. Drain and keep warm.

2 Heat the oil in a pan over a medium heat and fry the onions for 2–3 minutes or until soft. Stir in the garlic and cook for 1 minute. Stir in the tomatoes, oregano and tomato purée (paste).

3 Add the water and the reserved beans to the pan. Bring to the boil, cover, then simmer for about 45 minutes, or until the beans are almost tender.

4 Add the pasta to the pan and season to taste. Stir in the sun-dried tomatoes, bring back to the boil, partly cover and simmer for 10 minutes, or until the pasta is tender, but still firm to the bite.

5 Stir the herbs into the soup. Ladle the soup into warm serving bowls, sprinkle with Parmesan and serve.

## COOK'S TIP

Place the beans in a pan of cold water and bring to the boil. Remove from the heat and leave the beans to cool in the water. Drain and rinse before using.

# Minestrone with Pesto

This version of minestrone contains cannellini beans – these need to be soaked overnight, so prepare in advance.

## NUTRITIONAL INFORMATION

Calories . . . . . . .604   Sugars . . . . . . . . .3g
Protein . . . . . . . .26g   Fat . . . . . . . . . .45g
Carbohydrate . . .24g   Saturates . . . . . .11g

10–15 MINS    1¾ HOURS

### SERVES 6

I N G R E D I E N T S

175 g/6 oz/scant 1 cup dried cannellini
  beans, soaked overnight

2.5 litres/4 ½ pints/10 cups water or stock

1 large onion, chopped

1 leek, trimmed and sliced thinly

2 celery stalks, sliced very thinly

2 carrots, chopped

3 tbsp olive oil

2 tomatoes, peeled and chopped roughly

1 courgette (zucchini), trimmed and
  sliced thinly

2 potatoes, diced

90 g/3 oz elbow macaroni (or other small
  macaroni)

salt and pepper

4–6 tbsp freshly grated Parmesan, to serve

P E S T O

2 tbsp pine kernels (nuts)

5 tbsp olive oil

2 bunches basil, stems removed

4–6 garlic cloves, crushed

90 g /3 oz/ ½ cup Pecorino or Parmesan,
  grated

1 Drain the beans, rinse and put in a pan with the water or stock. Bring to the boil, cover and simmer for 1 hour.

2 Add the onion, leek, celery, carrots and oil. Cover and simmer for 4–5 minutes.

3 Add the tomatoes, courgette (zucchini), potatoes, macaroni and seasoning. Cover again and continue to simmer for about 30 minutes or until very tender.

4 Meanwhile, make the pesto. Fry the pine kernels (nuts) in 1 tablespoon of the oil until pale brown, then drain. Put the basil into a food processor or blender with the nuts and garlic. Process until well chopped. Alternatively, chop finely by hand and pound with a pestle and mortar. Gradually add the remaining oil until smooth. Turn into a bowl, add the cheese and seasoning, and mix thoroughly.

5 Stir 1½ tablespoons of the pesto into the soup until well blended. Simmer for a further 5 minutes and adjust the seasoning. Serve very hot, sprinkled with the cheese.

# Minestrone Soup

*Minestrone* translates as 'big soup' in Italian. It is made all over Italy, but this version comes from Livorno, a port on the western coast.

## NUTRITIONAL INFORMATION

Calories . . . . . . . .311   Sugars . . . . . . . . .8g
Protein . . . . . . . .12g   Fat . . . . . . . . . .19g
Carbohydrate . . .26g   Saturates . . . . . . .5g

 10 MINS     30 MINS

### SERVES 4

## I N G R E D I E N T S

1 tbsp olive oil

2 medium onions, chopped

2 cloves garlic, crushed

1 potato, peeled and cut into 1 cm/
    ½ inch cubes

1 carrot, peeled and cut into chunks

1 leek, sliced into rings

¼ green cabbage, shredded

1 stick celery, chopped

450 g/1 lb can chopped tomatoes

200 g/7 oz can flageolet (small navy)
    beans, drained and rinsed

600 ml/1 pint/2 ½ cups hot vegetable stock,
    diluted with 600 ml/1 pint/2 ½ cups
    boiling water

bouquet garni (2 bay leaves, 2 sprigs
    rosemary and 2 sprigs thyme, tied
together)

salt and pepper

freshly grated Parmesan cheese, to serve

1 Heat the olive oil in a large saucepan. Add the chopped onions and garlic and fry for about 5 minutes, stirring, or until the onions are soft and golden.

2 Add the prepared potato, carrot, leek, cabbage and celery to the saucepan. Cook for a further 2 minutes, stirring frequently, to coat all of the vegetables in the oil.

3 Add the tomatoes, flageolet (small navy) beans, hot vegetable stock and bouquet garni to the pan, stirring to mix. Leave the soup to simmer, covered, for 15–20 minutes or until all of the vegetables are just tender.

4 Remove the bouquet garni, season with salt and pepper to taste and serve with plenty of freshly grated Parmesan cheese.

# Vegetable & Bean Soup

This wonderful combination of cannellini beans, vegetables and vermicelli is made even richer by the addition of pesto and dried mushrooms.

## NUTRITIONAL INFORMATION

| | |
|---|---|
| Calories . . . . . . . .294 | Sugars . . . . . . . . .2g |
| Protein . . . . . . . .11g | Fat . . . . . . . . . .16g |
| Carbohydrate . . .30g | Saturates . . . . . . .2g |

 30 MINS      30 MINS

### SERVES 4

## I N G R E D I E N T S

1 small aubergine (eggplant)

2 large tomatoes

1 potato, peeled

1 carrot, peeled

1 leek

425 g/15 oz can cannellini beans

850 ml/1½ pints/3¾ cups hot vegetable
   stock

2 tsp dried basil

15 g/½ oz dried porcini mushrooms,
   soaked for 10 minutes in enough warm
   water to cover

50 g/1¾ oz/¼ cup vermicelli

3 tbsp pesto

freshly grated Parmesan cheese, to serve
   (optional)

1 Slice the aubergine (eggplant) into rings about 1 cm/½ inch thick, then cut each ring into 4.

2 Cut the tomatoes and potato into small dice. Cut the carrot into sticks, about 2.5 cm/1 inch long and cut the leek into rings.

3 Place the cannellini beans and their liquid in a large saucepan. Add the aubergine (eggplant), tomatoes, potatoes, carrot and leek, stirring to mix.

4 Add the stock to the pan and bring to the boil. Reduce the heat and leave to simmer for 15 minutes.

5 Add the basil, dried mushrooms and their soaking liquid and the vermicelli and simmer for 5 minutes or until all of the vegetables are tender.

6 Remove the pan from the heat and stir in the pesto.

7 Serve with freshly grated Parmesan cheese, if using.

# Pasta & Olive Omelette

Use any leftover cooked pasta you may have, such as penne, short-cut macaroni or shells, to make this fluffy omelette an instant success.

## NUTRITIONAL INFORMATION

Calories . . . . . . . 521   Sugars . . . . . . . . 3g
Protein . . . . . . . 18g   Fat . . . . . . . . . . 34g
Carbohydrate . . . 38g   Saturates . . . . . . 6g

 20 MINS     20 MINS

### SERVES 2

## INGREDIENTS

4 tbsp olive oil

1 small onion, chopped

1 fennel bulb, thinly sliced

125 g/4½ oz raw potato, diced and dried

1 garlic clove, chopped

4 eggs

1 tbsp chopped parsley

pinch of cayenne pepper

90 g/3 oz short pasta, cooked weight

1 tbsp stuffed green olives, halved, plus
   extra to garnish

salt and pepper

marjoram sprigs, to garnish

tomato salad, to serve

1 Heat 2 tablespoons of the oil in a heavy frying pan (skillet) over a low heat and fry the onion, fennel and potato for 8-10 minutes, stirring occasionally, until the potato is just tender. Do not allow it to break up. Stir in the garlic and cook for 1 minute. Remove the pan from the heat, lift out the vegetables with a slotted spoon and set aside. Rinse and dry the pan.

2 Break the eggs into a bowl and beat until frothy. Stir in the parsley and season with salt, pepper and cayenne.

3 Heat 1 tablespoon of the remaining oil in a pan over a medium heat. Pour in half of the beaten eggs, then add the cooked vegetables, the pasta and the olives. Pour on the remaining egg and cook until the sides begin to set.

4 Lift up the edges with a spatula to allow the uncooked egg to spread underneath. Continue cooking the omelette, shaking the pan occasionally, until the underside is golden brown.

5 Slide the omelette out on to a large, flat plate and wipe the pan clean with paper towels. Heat the remaining oil in the pan and invert the omelette. Cook the omelette on the other side until it is also golden brown.

6 Slide the omelette on to a warmed serving dish. Garnish with a few olives and sprigs of marjoram, and serve hot, cut into wedges, with a tomato salad, if wished.

# Marinated Aubergine

This unusual, fruity marinade makes the aubergine (eggplant) slices simply melt in the mouth.

## NUTRITIONAL INFORMATION

| | | | |
|---|---|---|---|
| Calories | . . . . . . 548 | Sugars | . . . . . . . 11g |
| Protein | . . . . . . . 15g | Fats | . . . . . . . . . 18g |
| Carbohydrate | . . 85g | Saturates | . . . . . . 3g |

2¼ HRS     25 MINS

## SERVES 4

## I N G R E D I E N T S

150 ml/¼ pint/⅝ cup
   vegetable stock

150 ml/¼ pint/⅝ cup white
   wine vinegar

2 tsp balsamic vinegar

3 tbsp olive oil

fresh oregano sprig

450 g/1 lb aubergine (eggplant), peeled and
   thinly sliced

400 g/14 oz dried linguine

### M A R I N A D E

2 tbsp extra virgin oil

2 garlic cloves, crushed

2 tbsp chopped fresh oregano

2 tbsp finely chopped
   roasted almonds

2 tbsp diced red (bell) pepper

2 tbsp lime juice

grated rind and juice of 1 orange

salt and pepper

1 Put the vegetable stock, wine vinegar and balsamic vinegar into a saucepan and bring to the boil over a low heat. Add 2 tsp of the olive oil and the sprig of oregano and simmer gently for about 1 minute.

2 Add the aubergine slices to the pan, remove from the heat and set aside for 10 minutes.

3 Meanwhile, make the marinade. Combine the oil, garlic, fresh oregano, almonds, (bell) pepper, lime juice, orange rind and juice and seasoning in a large bowl.

4 Remove the aubergine (eggplant) from the saucepan with a slotted spoon, and drain well. Mix the aubergine (eggplant) slices into the marinade. Leave to marinate in a refrigerator for at least 2 hours or overnight if possible.

5 Bring a pan of salted water to the boil. Add half the remaining oil and the linguine and cook until just tender. Drain the pasta and toss with the remaining oil. Arrange the pasta on a serving plate with the aubergine (eggplant) slices and the marinade and serve.

# Spinach & Ricotta Shells

This is a classic combination in which the smooth, creamy cheese balances the sharper taste of the spinach.

## NUTRITIONAL INFORMATION

Calories ...... 634  Sugars ........ 8g
Protein ....... 23g  Fats ......... 23g
Carbohydrate .. 89g  Saturates ...... 7g

  25 MINS  30 MINS

### SERVES 4

## I N G R E D I E N T S

400 g/14 oz dried lumache
   rigate grande

5 tbsp olive oil

60g/2 oz/1 cup fresh
   white breadcrumbs

125 ml/4 fl oz/½ cup milk

300 g/10½ oz frozen spinach, thawed and
   drained

225 g/8 oz/1 cup ricotta cheese

pinch of freshly grated nutmeg

400 g/14 oz can chopped
   tomatoes, drained

1 garlic clove, crushed

salt and pepper

## COOK'S TIP

Ricotta is a creamy Italian cheese traditionally made from ewes' milk whey. It is soft and white, with a smooth texture and a slightly sweet flavour. It should be used within 2–3 days of purchase.

 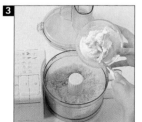 

1 Bring a large saucepan of lightly salted water to the boil. Add the lumache and 1 tbsp of the olive oil and cook until just tender, but still firm to the bite. Drain the pasta, refresh under cold water and set aside.

2 Put the breadcrumbs, milk and 3 tbsp of the remaining olive oil in a food processor and work to combine.

3 Add the spinach and ricotta cheese to the food processor and work to a smooth mixture. Transfer to a bowl, stir in the nutmeg, and season with salt and pepper to taste.

4 Mix together the tomatoes, garlic and remaining oil and spoon the mixture into the base of an ovenproof dish.

5 Using a teaspoon, fill the lumache with the spinach and ricotta mixture and arrange on top of the tomato mixture in the dish. Cover and bake in a preheated oven at 180°C/350°F/Gas 4 for 20 minutes. Serve hot.

# Baked Aubergines with Pasta

Combined with tomatoes and mozzarella cheese, pasta makes a tasty filling for baked aubergine (eggplant) shells.

## NUTRITIONAL INFORMATION

Calories ...... 451   Sugars ....... 18g
Protein ....... 17g   Fats ......... 18g
Carbohydrate .. 59g   Saturates ...... 5g

  15 MINS      50 MINS

### SERVES 4

## I N G R E D I E N T S

225 g/8 oz dried penne or other short pasta shapes

4 tbsp olive oil, plus extra for brushing

2 aubergines (eggplants)

1 large onion, chopped

2 garlic cloves, crushed

400 g/14 oz can chopped tomatoes

2 tsp dried oregano

60 g/2 oz mozzarella cheese, thinly sliced

25 g/1 oz/⅓ cup freshly grated Parmesan cheese

2 tbsp dry breadcrumbs

salt and pepper

salad leaves (greens), to serve

1 Bring a pan of salted water to the boil. Add the pasta and 1 tbsp of the olive oil and cook until tender. Drain, return to the pan, cover and keep warm.

2 Cut the aubergines (eggplants) in half lengthways and score around the inside, being careful not to pierce the shells. Scoop out the flesh then brush the insides of the shells with oil. Chop the flesh and set aside.

3 Fry the onion in the remaining oil until translucent. Add the garlic and fry for 1 minute. Stir in the chopped aubergine (eggplant) and fry for 5 minutes. Add the tomatoes, oregano and seasoning. Bring to the boil and simmer for 10 minutes. Remove from the heat and stir in the pasta.

4 Brush a baking (cookie) sheet with oil and arrange the aubergine (eggplant) shells in a single layer. Divide half the tomato and pasta mixture between them. Sprinkle over the mozzarella, then pile the remaining tomato and pasta mixture on top. Mix the Parmesan cheese and breadcrumbs and sprinkle over the top.

5 Bake in a preheated oven at 200°C/400°C/ Gas 6 for 25 minutes, until golden brown. Serve with salad leaves (greens).

# Tricolour Timballini

An unusual way of serving pasta, these cheese moulds are excellent with a crunchy salad for a light lunch.

## NUTRITIONAL INFORMATION

| | | | |
|---|---|---|---|
| Calories | 608 | Sugars | 17g |
| Protein | 21g | Fats | 30g |
| Carbohydrate | 63g | Saturates | 12g |

30 MINS · 50 MINS

### SERVES 4

## INGREDIENTS

15 g/½ oz/1 tbsp butter, softened

60 g/2 oz/1 cup dried white breadcrumbs

175 g/6 oz dried tricolour spaghetti, broken into 5 cm/2 inch lengths

3 tbsp olive oil

1 egg yolk

125 g/4 oz/1 cup grated Gruyère (Swiss) cheese

300 ml/½ pint/1¼ cups béchamel sauce

1 onion, finely chopped

1 bay leaf

150 ml/¼ pint/⅝ cup dry white wine

150 ml/¼ pint/⅝ cup passata (sieved tomatoes)

1 tbsp tomato purée (paste)

salt and pepper

fresh basil leaves, to garnish

1 Grease four 180 ml/6 fl oz/¾ cup ramekins with the butter. Evenly coat the insides with half the breadcrumbs.

2 Bring a pan of lightly salted water to the boil. Add the spaghetti and 1 tbsp of the oil and cook until just tender. Drain and transfer to a mixing bowl.

3 Add the egg yolk and cheese to the pasta and season. Pour the béchamel sauce into the bowl and mix. Spoon the mixture into the ramekins and sprinkle over the remaining breadcrumbs.

4 Stand the ramekins on a baking (cookie) sheet and bake in a preheated oven at 220°C/ 425°F/Gas 7 for 20 minutes. Set aside for 10 minutes.

5 To make the sauce, heat the remaining oil in a pan and gently fry the onion and bay leaf for 2-3 minutes.

6 Stir in the wine, passata (sieved tomatoes) and tomato purée (paste). Season and simmer for 20 minutes, until thickened. Discard the bay leaf.

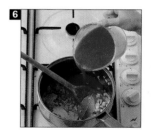

7 Turn the timballini out on to individual serving plates, garnish with the basil leaves and serve with the tomato sauce.

# Tagliarini with Gorgonzola

This simple, creamy pasta sauce is a classic Italian recipe.

## NUTRITIONAL INFORMATION

| | | | |
|---|---|---|---|
| Calories | 855 | Sugars | 5g |
| Protein | 19g | Fats | 52g |
| Carbohydrate | 80g | Saturates | 30g |

 10 MINS    25 MINS

**SERVES 4**

## I N G R E D I E N T S

25 g/1 oz/2 tbsp butter

225 g/8 oz Gorgonzola cheese, roughly crumbled

150 ml/¼ pint/⅝ cup double (heavy) cream

30 ml/2 tbsp dry white wine

1 tsp cornflour (cornstarch)

4 fresh sage sprigs, finely chopped

400 g/14 oz dried tagliarini

2 tbsp olive oil

salt and white pepper

fresh herb sprigs, to garnish

1 Melt the butter in a heavy-based saucepan. Stir in 175 g/6 oz of the Gorgonzola and melt, over a low heat, for 2 minutes.

2 Add the cream, wine and cornflour (cornstarch) and beat with a whisk until fully incorporated.

3 Stir in the sage and season to taste. Bring to the boil over a low heat, whisking constantly, until the sauce thickens. Remove from the heat and set aside.

4 Bring a large saucepan of lightly salted water to the boil. Add the tagliarini and 1 tbsp of the olive oil. Cook the pasta for 12–14 minutes or until just tender, drain thoroughly and toss in the remaining olive oil. Transfer the pasta to a serving dish and keep warm.

5 Reheat the sauce over a low heat, whisking constantly. Spoon the Gorgonzola sauce over the tagliarini, sprinkle over the remaining cheese, garnish and serve.

## COOK'S TIP

Gorgonzola is one of the world's oldest veined cheeses and, arguably, its finest. When buying, always check that it is creamy yellow with delicate green veining. Avoid hard or discoloured cheese. It should have a rich, piquant aroma, not a bitter smell. If you find Gorgonzola too strong or rich, you could substitute Danish blue.

# Three-Cheese Bake

Serve this dish while the cheese is still hot and melted as cooked cheese turns very rubbery if it is allowed to cool down.

## NUTRITIONAL INFORMATION

| | | | |
|---|---|---|---|
| Calories | 671 | Sugars | 5g |
| Protein | 34g | Fats | 28g |
| Carbohydrate | 77g | Saturates | 14g |

 10 MINS  55 MINS

### SERVES 4

## I N G R E D I E N T S

butter, for greasing

400 g/14 oz dried penne

1 tbsp olive oil

2 eggs, beaten

350 g/12 oz/1½ cups ricotta cheese

4 fresh basil sprigs

100 g/3¼ oz/1 cup grated mozzarella or halloumi cheese

4 tbsp freshly grated Parmesan cheese

salt and black pepper

fresh basil leaves (optional), to garnish

1 Lightly grease an ovenproof dish.

2 Bring a large pan of lightly salted water to the boil. Add the penne and olive oil and cook until just tender, but still firm to the bite. Drain the pasta, set aside and keep warm.

3 Beat the eggs into the ricotta cheese and season to taste with salt and pepper.

4 Spoon half of the penne into the base of the dish and cover with half of the basil leaves.

5 Spoon over half of the ricotta cheese mixture. Sprinkle over the mozzarella or halloumi cheese and top with the remaining basil leaves. Cover with the remaining penne and then spoon over the remaining ricotta cheese mixture. Lightly sprinkle over the grated Parmesan cheese.

6 Bake in a preheated oven at 190°C/375°F/ Gas 5 for about 30–40 minutes, until golden brown and the cheese topping is hot and bubbling. Garnish with fresh basil leaves, if liked, and serve hot.

## VARIATION

Try substituting smoked Bavarian cheese for the mozzarella or halloumi and grated Cheddar cheese for the Parmesan, for a slightly different but just as delicious flavour.

# Pasta & Bean Casserole

A satisfying winter dish, pasta and bean casserole with a crunchy topping is a slow-cooked, one-pot meal.

## NUTRITIONAL INFORMATION

| | | | |
|---|---|---|---|
| Calories | 416 | Sugars | 9g |
| Protein | 16g | Fats | 13g |
| Carbohydrate | 61g | Saturates | 2g |

 15 MINS   3¼–3½ HRS

### SERVES 6

## I N G R E D I E N T S

225 g/8 oz/1¼ cups dried haricot (navy) beans, soaked overnight and drained

225 g/8 oz dried penne

6 tbsp olive oil

850 ml/1½ pints /3½ cups vegetable stock

2 large onions, sliced

2 garlic cloves, chopped

2 bay leaves

1 tsp dried oregano

1 tsp dried thyme

5 tbsp red wine

2 tbsp tomato purée (paste)

2 celery sticks (stalks), sliced

1 fennel bulb, sliced

115 g/4 oz/1⅝ cups sliced mushrooms

250 g/8 oz tomatoes, sliced

1 tsp dark muscovado sugar

4 tbsp dry white breadcrumbs

salt and pepper

salad leaves (greens) and crusty bread, to serve

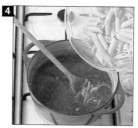

1 Put the haricot (navy) beans in a large saucepan and add cold water to cover. Bring to the boil and boil vigorously for 20 minutes. Drain, set aside and keep warm.

2 Bring a large saucepan of lightly salted water to the boil. Add the penne and 1 tbsp of the olive oil and cook for about 3 minutes. Drain the pasta, set aside and keep warm.

3 Put the beans in a large, flameproof casserole. Add the vegetable stock and stir in the remaining olive oil, the onions, garlic, bay leaves, oregano, thyme, wine and tomato purée (paste). Bring to the boil, then cover and cook in a preheated oven at 180°C/350°F/Gas 4 for 2 hours.

4 Add the penne, celery, fennel, mushrooms and tomatoes to the casserole and season to taste with salt and pepper. Stir in the muscovado sugar and sprinkle over the breadcrumbs. Cover the dish and cook in the oven for 1 further hour.

5 Serve hot with salad leaves (greens) and crusty bread.

# Pasta-Stuffed Tomatoes

This unusual and inexpensive dish would make a good starter for eight people or a delicious lunch for four.

## NUTRITIONAL INFORMATION

| | | | |
|---|---|---|---|
| Calories | 350 | Sugars | 10g |
| Protein | 12g | Fats | 21g |
| Carbohydrate | 31g | Saturates | 6g |

 15 MINS     30 MINS

### SERVES 4

## I N G R E D I E N T S

5 tbsp extra virgin olive oil, plus extra for greasing

8 beef tomatoes or large round tomatoes

115 g/4 oz/1 cup dried ditalini or other very small pasta shapes

8 black olives, stoned (pitted) and finely chopped

2 tbsp finely chopped fresh basil

1 tbsp finely chopped fresh parsley

60 g/2 oz/⅔ cup freshly grated Parmesan cheese

salt and pepper

fresh basil sprigs, to garnish

1 Brush a baking (cookie) sheet with olive oil.

2 Slice the tops off the tomatoes and reserve to make 'lids'. If the tomatoes will not stand up, cut a thin slice off the bottom of each tomato.

3 Scoop out the tomato pulp into a strainer, but do not pierce the tomato shells. Invert the tomato shells, pat dry and then set aside to drain.

4 Bring a large pan of lightly salted water to the boil. Add the pasta and 1 tbsp of the remaining olive oil and cook until tender, but still firm to the bite. Drain and set aside.

5 Put the olives, chopped basil, parsley and Parmesan cheese into a large mixing bowl and stir in the drained tomato pulp. Add the pasta to the bowl. Stir in the remaining olive oil and season to taste with salt and pepper.

6 Spoon the pasta mixture into the tomato shells and replace the lids. Arrange the tomatoes on the baking (cookie) sheet and bake in a preheated oven at 190°C/375°F/Gas 5 for 15–20 minutes.

7 Remove the tomatoes from the oven and allow to cool until just warm. Arrange on a serving dish, garnish with the fresh basil sprigs and serve.

# Pasta & Garlic Mayo Salad

This crisp salad would make an excellent accompaniment to a variety of summer dishes.

## NUTRITIONAL INFORMATION

Calories . . . . . . .858  Sugars . . . . . . . .35g
Protein . . . . . . . .11g  Fat . . . . . . . . . .64g
Carbohydrate . . .64g  Saturates . . . . . . .8g

1½ HOURS        10 MINS

**SERVES 4**

## I N G R E D I E N T S

2 large lettuces

260 g/9 oz dried penne

1 tbsp olive oil

8 red eating apples

juice of 4 lemons

1 head of celery, sliced

115 g/4 oz/¾ cup shelled, halved walnuts

250 ml/9 fl oz/1⅛ cups fresh garlic
   mayonnaise (see Cook's Tip)

salt

1 Wash, drain and pat dry the lettuce leaves with kitchen paper. Transfer them to the refrigerator for 1 hour or until crisp.

2 Meanwhile, bring a large saucepan of lightly salted water to the boil. Add the pasta and olive oil and cook for 8–10 minutes or until tender, but still firm to the bite. Drain the pasta and refresh under cold running water. Drain thoroughly again and set aside.

3 Core and dice the apples, place them in a small bowl and sprinkle with the lemon juice.

4 Mix together the pasta, celery, apples and walnuts and toss the mixture in the garlic mayonnaise (see Cook's Tip). Add more mayonnaise, if liked.

5 Line a salad bowl with the lettuce leaves and spoon the pasta salad into the lined bowl. Serve when required.

## COOK'S TIP

To make garlic mayo, beat 2 egg yolks with a pinch of salt and 6 crushed garlic cloves. Start beating in 350ml/12 fl oz/1½ cups oil, 1–2 tsp at a time. When ¼ of the oil has been incorporated, beat in 1–2 tbsp white wine vinegar. Continue beating in the oil. Stir in 1 tsp Dijon mustard and season.

# Goat's Cheese & Penne Salad

This superb salad is delicious on its own or when served as a side dish.

## NUTRITIONAL INFORMATION

| | | | |
|---|---|---|---|
| Calories | .......634 | Sugars | ........13g |
| Protein | ........18g | Fat | ..........51g |
| Carbohydrate | ...27g | Saturates | ......13g |

1¹/₂ HOURS     15 MINS

### SERVES 4

## I N G R E D I E N T S

250 g/9 oz dried penne

5 tbsp olive oil

1 head radicchio, torn into pieces

1 Webbs lettuce, torn into pieces

7 tbsp chopped walnuts

2 ripe pears, cored and diced

1 fresh basil sprig

1 bunch of watercress, trimmed

2 tbsp lemon juice

3 tbsp garlic vinegar

4 tomatoes, quartered

1 small onion, sliced

1 large carrot, grated

250 g/9 oz goat's cheese, diced

salt and pepper

1 Bring a large saucepan of lightly salted water to the boil. Add the penne and 1 tablespoon of the olive oil and cook for 8–10 minutes or until tender, but still firm to the bite. Drain the pasta, refresh under cold running water, drain thoroughly again and set aside to cool.

2 Place the radicchio and Webbs lettuce in a large salad bowl and mix together well. Top with the pasta, walnuts, pears, basil and watercress.

3 Mix together the lemon juice, the remaining olive oil and the vinegar in a measuring jug (pitcher). Pour the mixture over the salad ingredients and toss to coat the salad leaves well.

4 Add the tomato quarters, onion slices, grated carrot and diced goat's cheese and toss together, using 2 forks, until well mixed. Leave the salad to chill in the refrigerator for about 1 hour before serving.

## COOK'S TIP

Radiccio is a variety of chicory (endive) originating in Italy. It has a slightly bitter flavour.

# Pasta Salad & Basil Vinaigrette

All the ingredients of pesto sauce are included in this salad, which has a fabulous summery taste, perfect for *al fresco* eating.

## NUTRITIONAL INFORMATION

| | | | |
|---|---|---|---|
| Calories | .......432 | Sugars | .........3g |
| Protein | ........14g | Fat | ..........29g |
| Carbohydrate | ...30g | Saturates | .......6g |

25 MINS    15 MINS

### SERVES 4

## INGREDIENTS

225 g/8 oz fusilli

4 tomatoes

50 g/1 ¾ oz black olives

25 g/1 oz sun-dried tomatoes in oil

2 tbsp pine nuts

2 tbsp grated Parmesan cheese

fresh basil, to garnish

### VINAIGRETTE

15 g/½ oz basil leaves

1 clove garlic

2 tbsp grated Parmesan cheese

4 tbsp extra virgin olive oil

2 tbsp lemon juice

salt and pepper

### COOK'S TIP

Sun-dried tomatoes have a strong, intense flavour. They are most frequently found packed in oil with herbs and garlic. Do not waste the oil, which has an excellent flavour, instead use it in salad dressings.

1 Cook the pasta in a saucepan of lightly salted boiling water for 8–10 minutes or until just tender. Drain the pasta, rinse under cold water, then drain again thoroughly. Place the pasta in a large bowl.

2 To make the vinaigrette, place the basil leaves, garlic, cheese, oil and lemon juice in a food processor. Season with salt and pepper to taste. Process until the leaves are well chopped and the ingredients are combined. Alternatively, finely chop the basil leaves by hand and combine with the other vinaigrette ingredients. Pour the vinaigrette over the pasta and toss to coat.

3 Cut the tomatoes into wedges. Pit and halve the olives. Slice the sun-dried tomatoes. Place the pine nuts on a baking tray (cookie sheet) and toast under the grill (broiler) until golden.

4 Add the tomatoes (fresh and sun-dried) and the olives to the pasta and mix.

5 Transfer the pasta to a serving dish, scatter over the Parmesan and pine nuts and garnish with a few basil leaves.

# Cheese, Nut & Pasta Salad

Use colourful salad leaves (greens) to provide visual contrast to match the contrasts of taste and texture.

### NUTRITIONAL INFORMATION

| | |
|---|---|
| Calories . . . . . . . .694 | Sugars . . . . . . . . .1g |
| Protein . . . . . . . .22g | Fat . . . . . . . . . .57g |
| Carbohydrate . . .24g | Saturates . . . . . .15g |

15 MINS     15–20 MINS

### SERVES 4

## I N G R E D I E N T S

225 g/8 oz/2 cups dried pasta shells

1 tbsp olive oil

115 g/4 oz/1 cup shelled and
  halved walnuts

mixed salad leaves (greens), such as
  radicchio, escarole, rocket (arugula),
  lamb's lettuce (corn salad) and frisée

225 g/8 oz dolcelatte cheese, crumbled

salt

### D R E S S I N G

2 tbsp walnut oil

4 tbsp extra virgin olive oil

2 tbsp red wine vinegar

salt and pepper

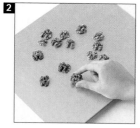  

1 Bring a large saucepan of lightly salted water to the boil. Add the pasta shells and olive oil and cook for 8–10 minutes or until just tender, but still firm to the bite. Drain the pasta, refresh under cold running water, drain thoroughly again and set aside.

2 Spread out the shelled walnut halves on to a baking tray (cookie sheet) and toast under a preheated grill (broiler) for 2–3 minutes. Set aside to cool while you make the dressing.

3 To make the dressing, whisk together the walnut oil, olive oil and vinegar in a small bowl, and season to taste.

4 Arrange the salad leaves (greens) in a large serving bowl. Pile the cooled pasta in the middle of the salad leaves (greens) and sprinkle over the dolcelatte cheese. Pour the dressing over the pasta salad, scatter over the walnut halves and toss together to mix. Serve immediately.

### COOK'S TIP

Dolcelatte is a semi-soft, blue-veined cheese from Italy. Its texture is creamy and smooth and the flavour is delicate, but piquant. You could use Roquefort instead. It is essential that whatever cheese you choose, it is of the best quality and in peak condition.

# Italian Pasta Salad

Tomatoes and mozzarella cheese are a classic Italian combination. Here they are joined with pasta and avocado for an extra touch of luxury.

## NUTRITIONAL INFORMATION

| | |
|---|---|
| Calories . . . . . . . .541 | Sugars . . . . . . . . .5g |
| Protein . . . . . . . .12g | Fat . . . . . . . . . .43g |
| Carbohydrate . . .29g | Saturates . . . . . .10g |

15 MINS    15 MINS

### SERVES 4

## INGREDIENTS

2 tbsp pine nuts (kernels)

175 g/6 oz/1½ cups dried fusilli

1 tbsp olive oil

6 tomatoes

225 g/8 oz mozzarella cheese

1 large avocado pear

2 tbsp lemon juice

3 tbsp chopped fresh basil

salt and pepper

fresh basil sprigs, to garnish

### DRESSING

6 tbsp extra virgin olive oil

2 tbsp white wine vinegar

1 tsp wholegrain mustard

pinch of sugar

1 Spread the pine nuts (kernels) out on a baking tray (cookie sheet) and toast them under a preheated grill (broiler) for 1–2 minutes. Remove and set aside to cool.

2 Bring a large saucepan of lightly salted water to the boil. Add the fusilli and olive oil and cook for 8–10 minutes or until tender, but still firm to the bite. Drain the pasta and refresh in cold water. Drain again and set aside to cool.

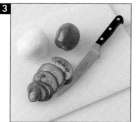 

3 Thinly slice the tomatoes and the mozzarella cheese.

4 Cut the avocado pear in half, then carefully remove the stone (pit) and skin. Cut into thin slices lengthways and sprinkle with lemon juice to prevent discoloration.

5 To make the dressing, whisk together the oil, vinegar, mustard and sugar in a small bowl, and season to taste with salt and pepper.

6 Arrange the tomatoes, mozzarella cheese and avocado pear alternately in overlapping slices on to a large serving platter.

7 Toss the pasta with half of the dressing and the chopped basil and season to taste with salt and pepper. Spoon the pasta into the centre of the platter and pour over the remaining dressing. Sprinkle over the pine nuts (kernels), garnish with fresh basil sprigs and serve immediately.

# Pasta with Pesto Vinaigrette

Sun-dried tomatoes and olives enhance this delicious pesto-inspired salad, which is just as tasty served cold.

## NUTRITIONAL INFORMATION

Calories . . . . . . .275   Sugars . . . . . . . . .2g
Protein . . . . . . . . .9g   Fat . . . . . . . . . .19g
Carbohydrate . . .17g   Saturates . . . . . . .4g

 35–40 MINS    15 MINS

### SERVES 6

## I N G R E D I E N T S

225 g/8 oz pasta spirals

4 tomatoes, skinned

60 g/2 oz/½ cup black olives

25 g/1 oz/¼ cup sun-dried tomatoes

2 tbsp pine kernels (nuts), toasted

2 tbsp Parmesan shavings

sprig of fresh basil, to garnish

### P E S T O   V I N A I G R E T T E

4 tbsp chopped fresh basil

1 garlic clove, crushed

2 tbsp freshly grated Parmesan

4 tbsp olive oil

2 tbsp lemon juice

pepper

1 Cook the pasta in a saucepan of boiling salted water for 8–10 minutes or until al dente. Drain the pasta and rinse well in hot water, then drain again thoroughly.

2 To make the vinaigrette, whisk the basil, garlic, Parmesan, olive oil, lemon juice and pepper until well blended.

3 Put the pasta into a bowl, pour over the basil vinaigrette and toss thoroughly.

4 Cut the tomatoes into wedges. Halve and pit the olives and slice the sun-dried tomatoes.

5 Add the tomatoes, olives and sun-dried tomatoes to the pasta and mix.

6 Transfer to a salad bowl and scatter the nuts and Parmesan shavings over the top. Serve warm, garnished with a sprig of basil.

# Cherry Tomato & Pasta Salad

Pasta tastes perfect in this lively salad, dressed with red wine vinegar, lemon juice, basil and olive oil.

## NUTRITIONAL INFORMATION

| | | | |
|---|---|---|---|
| Calories | .......228 | Sugars | .........4g |
| Protein | .........5g | Fat | ..........12g |
| Carbohydrate | ...27g | Saturates | .......2g |

  50 MINS    20 MINS

### SERVES 4

## INGREDIENTS

175 g/6 oz/1½ cups pasta shapes

1 yellow (bell) pepper, halved,
  cored and deseeded

2 small courgettes (zucchini), sliced

1 red onion, sliced thinly

125 g/4½ oz cherry tomatoes, halved

a handful of fresh basil leaves, torn into
  small pieces

salt

sprigs of fresh basil, to garnish

### DRESSING

4 tbsp olive oil

2 tbsp red wine vinegar

2 tsp lemon juice

1 tsp mustard

½ tsp caster (superfine) sugar

salt and pepper

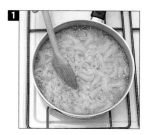

1 Cook the pasta in a pan of boiling, lightly salted water for 8–10 minutes, or until just tender.

2 Meanwhile, place the (bell) pepper halves, skin-side uppermost, under a preheated grill (broiler) until they just begin to char. Leave them to cool, then peel and slice them into strips.

3 Cook the courgettes (zucchini) in a small amount of boiling, lightly salted water for 3–4 minutes, until cooked, yet still crunchy. Drain and refresh under cold running water to cool quickly.

4 To make the dressing, mix together the olive oil, red wine vinegar, lemon juice, mustard and sugar. Season well with salt and pepper. Add the basil leaves.

5 Drain the pasta well and tip it into a large serving bowl. Add the dressing and toss well. Add the pepper, courgettes (zucchini), onion and cherry tomatoes, stirring to combine. Cover and leave at room temperature for about 30 minutes to allow the flavours to develop.

6 Serve, garnished with a few sprigs of fresh basil.

# Mushroom & Pasta Flan

Lightly cooked vermicelli is baked with a creamy mushroom filling to make this delicious flan.

## NUTRITIONAL INFORMATION

| | |
|---|---|
| Calories .......557 | Sugars .........5g |
| Protein ........15g | Fat ..........36g |
| Carbohydrate ...47g | Saturates ......19g |

🍲 10 MINS    🕐 1 HR 10 MINS

### SERVES 4

## I N G R E D I E N T S

225 g/8 oz vermicelli or spaghetti

1 tbsp olive oil

25 g/1 oz/2 tbsp butter, plus extra for
    greasing

salt and pepper

tomato and basil salad, to serve

### S A U C E

60 g/2 oz/¼ cup butter

1 onion, chopped

150 g/5½ oz button mushrooms, trimmed

1 green (bell) pepper, cored, deseeded and
    sliced into thin rings

150 ml/¼ pint/⅔ cup milk

3 eggs, beaten lightly

2 tbsp double (heavy) cream

1 tsp dried oregano

pinch of finely grated nutmeg

1 tbsp freshly grated Parmesan

1 Cook the pasta in a large pan of salted boiling water, adding the olive oil, for 8–10 minutes or until tender. Drain the pasta in a colander, return to the pan, add the butter and shake the pan well.

2 Grease a 20 cm/8 inch loose-bottomed flan tin (pan). Press the pasta on to the base and around the sides to form a case.

3 Heat the butter in a frying pan (skillet) over a medium heat and fry the onion until it is translucent. Remove with a slotted spoon and spread in the flan base.

4 Add the mushrooms and (bell) pepper rings to the pan and turn them in the fat until glazed. Fry for 2 minutes on each side, then arrange in the flan base.

5 Beat together the milk, eggs and cream, stir in the oregano, and season with nutmeg and pepper. Pour the mixture carefully over the vegetables and sprinkle on the cheese.

6 Bake the flan in the preheated oven, 180°C/350°F/Gas Mark 4, for 40–45 minutes, or until the filling is set. Slide on to a serving plate and serve warm.

# Beetroot Cannolicchi

Quick and simple, this colourful, warm salad works equally well as a tasty starter or as a main dish.

## NUTRITIONAL INFORMATION

| | | |
|---|---|---|
| Calories .......449 | Sugars ........13g | |
| Protein ........12g | Fat ..........15g | |
| Carbohydrate ...70g | Saturates ......2g | |

 10 MINS    20 MINS

### SERVES 4

## I N G R E D I E N T S

300 g/11 oz dried ditalini rigati

5 tbsp olive oil

2 garlic cloves, chopped

400 g/14 oz can chopped tomatoes

400 g/14 oz cooked beetroot (beet), diced

2 tbsp chopped fresh basil leaves

1 tsp mustard seeds

salt and pepper

### T O   S E R V E

mixed salad leaves (greens), tossed in olive oil

4 Italian plum tomatoes, sliced

1 Bring a large pan of salted water to the boil. Add the pasta and 1 tbsp of the oil and cook for about 10 minutes, until tender, but still firm to the bite. Drain and set aside.

2 Heat the remaining oil in a large saucepan and fry the garlic for 3 minutes. Add the chopped tomatoes and cook for 10 minutes.

3 Remove the pan from the heat and carefully add the beetroot (beet), basil, mustard seeds and pasta and season to taste with salt and black pepper.

4 Serve on a bed of mixed salad leaves (greens) tossed in olive oil, and sliced plum tomatoes.

## COOK'S TIP

To cook raw beetroot (beet), trim off the leaves about 5 cm/2 inches above the root and ensure that the skin is not broken. Boil in very lightly salted water for 30–40 minutes, until tender. Leave to cool and rub off the skin.

# Penne & Vegetables

The sweet cherry tomatoes in this recipe add colour and flavour and are complemented by the black olives and (bell) peppers.

## NUTRITIONAL INFORMATION

| | |
|---|---|
| Calories . . . . . . .380 | Sugars . . . . . . . . .6g |
| Protein . . . . . . . . .8g | Fat . . . . . . . . . .16g |
| Carbohydrate . . .48g | Saturates . . . . . . .7g |

 10 MINS   25 MINS

### SERVES 4

## INGREDIENTS

225 g/8 oz/2 cups dried penne

2 tbsp olive oil

25 g/1 oz/2 tbsp butter

2 garlic cloves, crushed

1 green (bell) pepper, seeded and
    thinly sliced

1 yellow (bell) pepper, seeded and
    thinly sliced

16 cherry tomatoes, halved

1 tbsp chopped oregano

125 ml/4 fl oz/½ cup dry white wine

2 tbsp quartered, pitted black olives

75 g/2¾ oz/1 bunch rocket (arugula)

salt and pepper

oregano sprigs, to garnish

## VARIATION

If rocket (arugula) is unavailable, spinach makes a good substitute. Follow the same cooking instructions as for rocket (arugula).

1 Cook the pasta in a saucepan of boiling salted water for 8–10 minutes or until al dente. Drain thoroughly.

2 Heat the oil and butter in a pan until the butter melts. Sauté the garlic for 30 seconds. Add the (bell) peppers and cook, stirring, for 3–4 minutes.

3 Stir in the cherry tomatoes, oregano, wine and olives and cook for 3–4 minutes. Season well with salt and pepper and stir in the rocket (arugula) until just wilted.

4 Transfer the pasta to a serving dish, spoon over the sauce and garnish.

# Spinach & Nut Pasta

Use any pasta shapes that you have for this recipe. Multi-coloured tricolore pasta is visually the most attractive to use.

## NUTRITIONAL INFORMATION

| | | | |
|---|---|---|---|
| Calories | . . . . . . .603 | Sugars | . . . . . . . . .5g |
| Protein | . . . . . . . .12g | Fat | . . . . . . . . . .41g |
| Carbohydrate | . . .46g | Saturates | . . . . . . .6g |

 5 MINS       15 MINS

### SERVES 4

## INGREDIENTS

225 g/8 oz/2 cups dried pasta shapes

125 ml/4 fl oz/½ cup olive oil

2 garlic cloves, crushed

1 onion, quartered and sliced

3 large flat mushrooms, sliced

225 g/8 oz spinach

2 tbsp pine nuts

75 ml/3 fl oz/6 tbsp dry white wine

salt and pepper

Parmesan shavings, to garnish

1 Cook the pasta in a saucepan of boiling salted water for 8–10 minutes, or until al dente. Drain well.

2 Meanwhile, heat the oil in a large saucepan and sauté the garlic and onion for 1 minute.

## COOK'S TIP

Grate a little nutmeg over the dish for extra flavour, as this spice has a particular affinity with spinach.

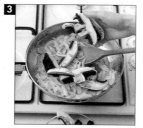

3 Add the sliced mushrooms to the pan and cook over a medium heat, stirring occasionally, for 2 minutes.

4 Lower the heat, add the spinach to the pan and cook, stirring occasionally, for 4–5 minutes, or until the spinach has wilted.

5 Stir in the pine nuts and wine, season to taste with salt and pepper and cook for 1 minute.

6 Transfer the pasta to a warm serving bowl and toss the sauce into it, mixing well. Garnish with shavings of Parmesan cheese and serve.

# Summertime Tagliatelle

This is a really fresh-tasting dish, made with courgettes (zucchini) and cream, which is ideal with a crisp white wine and some crusty bread.

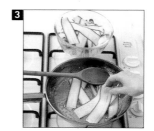

## NUTRITIONAL INFORMATION

| | |
|---|---|
| Calories .......502 | Sugars .........5g |
| Protein ........16g | Fat ..........30g |
| Carbohydrate ...44g | Saturates .......9g |

10 MINS     20 MINS

### SERVES 4

## INGREDIENTS

650 g/1½ lb courgettes (zucchini)

6 tbsp olive oil

3 garlic cloves, crushed

3 tbsp chopped basil

2 red chillies, sliced

juice of 1 large lemon

5 tbsp single (light) cream

4 tbsp grated Parmesan cheese

225 g/8 oz dried tagliatelle

salt and pepper

crusty bread, to serve

1 Using a swivel vegetable peeler, slice the courgettes (zucchini) into thin ribbons.

2 Heat the oil in a frying pan (skillet) and sauté the garlic for 30 seconds.

3 Add the courgette (zucchini) ribbons and cook over a low heat, stirring constantly, for 5–7 minutes.

4 Stir in the basil, chillies, lemon juice, single (light) cream and grated Parmesan cheese and season with salt and pepper to taste. Keep warm over a very low heat.

5 Meanwhile, cook the tagliatelle in a large pan of lightly salted boiling water for 10 minutes until al dente. Drain the pasta thoroughly and put in a warm serving bowl.

6 Pile the courgette (zucchini) mixture on top of the pasta. Serve immediately with crusty bread.

## COOK'S TIP

Lime juice could be used instead of the lemon. As limes are usually smaller, squeeze the juice from two.

# Vegetable Pasta Stir-Fry

East meets West in this delicious dish. Prepare all the vegetables and cook the pasta in advance, then the dish can be cooked in a few minutes.

## NUTRITIONAL INFORMATION

Calories . . . . . . .383    Sugars . . . . . . . .18g
Protein . . . . . . . .14g    Fat . . . . . . . . . .23g
Carbohydrate . . .32g    Saturates . . . . . . .8g

20 MINS          30 MINS

### SERVES 4

## INGREDIENTS

400 g/14 oz/4⅔ cups dried wholewheat
   pasta shells, or other short pasta shapes

1 tbsp olive oil

2 carrots, thinly sliced

115 g/4 oz baby corn cobs

3 tbsp peanut oil

2.5-cm/1-inch piece fresh ginger root,
   thinly sliced

1 large onion, thinly sliced

1 garlic clove, thinly sliced

3 celery sticks, thinly sliced

1 small red (bell) pepper, seeded and sliced
   into matchstick strips

1 small green (bell) pepper,
   seeded and sliced into matchstick strips

salt

steamed mangetouts (snow peas),
   to serve

### SAUCE

1 tsp cornflour (cornstarch)

2 tbsp water

3 tbsp soy sauce

3 tbsp dry sherry

1 tsp clear honey

dash of hot pepper sauce (optional)

1 Cook the pasta in a large pan of boiling lightly salted water, adding the tablespoon of olive oil. When tender, but still firm to the bite, drain the pasta in a colander, return to the pan, cover and keep warm.

2 Cook the carrots and baby corn cobs in boiling, salted water for 2 minutes. Drain in a colander, plunge into cold water to prevent further cooking and drain again.

3 Heat the peanut oil in a large frying pan (skillet) over medium heat. Add the ginger and stir-fry for 1 minute, to flavour the oil. Remove with a slotted spoon and discard.

4 Add the onion, garlic, celery and (bell) peppers to the oil and stir-fry over a medium heat for 2 minutes. Add the carrots and baby corn cobs, and stir-fry for a further 2 minutes, then stir in the reserved pasta.

5 Put the cornflour (cornstarch) in a small bowl and mix to a smooth paste with the water. Stir in the soy sauce, sherry and honey.

6 Pour the sauce into the pan, stir well and cook for 2 minutes, stirring once or twice. Taste the sauce and season with hot pepper sauce if wished. Serve with a steamed green vegetable, such as mangetouts (snow peas).

# Pasta Provençale

A Mediterranean mixture of red (bell) peppers, garlic and courgettes (zucchini) cooked in olive oil and tossed with pasta.

## NUTRITIONAL INFORMATION

| | | | |
|---|---|---|---|
| Calories | ......487 | Sugars | ........14g |
| Protein | ........17g | Fat | .........24g |
| Carbohydrate | ...53g | Saturates | .......8g |

5 MINS     20 MINS

### SERVES 4

## I N G R E D I E N T S

3 tbsp olive oil

1 onion, sliced

2 garlic cloves, chopped

3 red (bell) peppers, seeded
   and cut into strips

3 courgettes (zucchini), sliced

400 g/14 oz can chopped tomatoes

3 tbsp sun-dried tomato paste

2 tbsp chopped fresh basil

225 g/8 oz fresh pasta spirals

125 g/4½ oz/1 cup grated Gruyère cheese

salt and pepper

fresh basil sprigs, to garnish

1 Heat the oil in a heavy-based saucepan or flameproof casserole. Add the onion and garlic and cook, stirring occasionally, until softened. Add the (bell) peppers and courgettes (zucchini) and fry , stirring occasionally, for 5 minutes.

2 Add the tomatoes, sun-dried tomato paste and basil and season to taste with salt and pepper. Cover and cook for a further 5 minutes.

3 Meanwhile, bring a large saucepan of salted water to the boil and add the pasta. Stir and bring back to the boil.

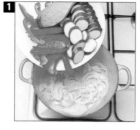

Reduce the heat slightly and cook, uncovered, for 3 minutes, until just tender. Drain thoroughly and add to the vegetables. Toss gently to mix well.

4 Transfer to a shallow flameproof dish and sprinkle with the cheese.

5 Cook under a preheated grill (broiler) for 5 minutes, until the cheese is golden brown and bubbling. Garnish with basil sprigs and serve immediately.

# Lemony Spaghetti

Steaming vegetables helps to preserve their nutritional content and allows them to retain their bright, natural colours and crunchy texture.

## NUTRITIONAL INFORMATION

Calories .......133    Sugars .........8g
Protein .........8g    Fat ..........1g
Carbohydrate ...25g    Saturates .....0.2g

10 MINS        25 MINS

### SERVES 4

## I N G R E D I E N T S

225 g/8 oz celeriac

2 medium carrots

2 medium leeks

1 small red (bell) pepper

1 small yellow (bell) pepper

2 garlic cloves

1 tsp celery seeds

1 tbsp lemon juice

300 g/10½ oz spaghetti

celery leaves, chopped, to garnish

### L E M O N   D R E S S I N G

1 tsp finely grated lemon rind

1 tbsp lemon juice

4 tbsp low-fat natural fromage frais
   (unsweetened yogurt)

salt and pepper

2 tbsp snipped fresh chives

1 Peel the celeriac and carrots, cut into thin matchsticks and place in a bowl. Trim and slice the leeks, rinse under running water to flush out any trapped dirt, then shred finely. Halve, deseed and slice the (bell) peppers. Peel and thinly slice the garlic.

2 Add all of the vegetables to the bowl with the celeriac and the carrots.

Toss the vegetables with the celery seeds and lemon juice.

3 Bring a large saucepan of water to the boil and cook the spaghetti according to the instructions on the packet. Drain and keep warm.

4 Meanwhile, bring another large saucepan of water to the boil, put the vegetables in a steamer or sieve (strainer) and place over the boiling water. Cover and steam for 6–7 minutes or until tender.

5 While the spaghetti and vegetables are cooking, mix the ingredients for the lemon dressing together.

6 Transfer the spaghetti and vegetables to a warm serving bowl and mix with the dressing. Garnish with chopped celery leaves and serve.

# Vegetable Ravioli

It is important not to overcook the vegetable filling or it will become sloppy and unexciting, instead of firm to the bite and delicious.

## NUTRITIONAL INFORMATION

| | | | |
|---|---|---|---|
| Calories | . . . . . . .622 | Sugars | . . . . . . . .10g |
| Protein | . . . . . . . .12g | Fat | . . . . . . . . . .40g |
| Carbohydrate | . . .58g | Saturates | . . . . . . .6g |

1½ HOURS     55 MINS

### SERVES 4

## I N G R E D I E N T S

450 g/1 lb Basic Pasta Dough (see page 5)

1 tbsp olive oil

90 g/3 oz/6 tbsp butter

150 ml/5 fl oz/⅝ cup single (light) cream

75 g/3 oz/1 cup freshly grated
　Parmesan cheese

fresh basil sprigs, to garnish

### S T U F F I N G

2 large aubergines (eggplant)

3 large courgettes (zucchini)

6 large tomatoes

1 large green (bell) pepper

1 large red (bell) pepper

3 garlic cloves

1 large onion

125 ml/4 fl oz/½ cup olive oil

60 g/2 oz tomato purée (paste)

½ tsp chopped fresh basil

salt and pepper

1 To make the stuffing, cut the aubergines (eggplant) and courgettes (zucchini) into 2.5 cm/1 inch chunks. Put the aubergine (eggplant) pieces in a colander, sprinkle with salt and set aside for 20 minutes. Rinse and drain.

2 Blanch the tomatoes in boiling water for 2 minutes. Drain, skin and chop the flesh. Core and seed the (bell) peppers and cut into 2.5 cm/1 inch dice. Chop the garlic and onion.

3 Heat the oil in a saucepan. Add the garlic and onion and fry for 3 minutes.

4 Stir in the aubergines (eggplant), courgettes (zucchini), tomatoes, (bell) peppers, tomato purée (paste) and basil. Season with salt and pepper to taste, cover and simmer for 20 minutes, stirring frequently.

5 Roll out the pasta dough and cut out 7.5 cm/3 inch rounds with a plain cutter. Put a spoonful of the vegetable stuffing on each round. Dampen the edges slightly and fold the pasta rounds over, pressing together to seal.

6 Bring a saucepan of salted water to the boil. Add the ravioli and the oil and cook for 3–4 minutes. Drain and transfer to a greased ovenproof dish, dotting each layer with butter. Pour over the cream and sprinkle over the Parmesan cheese. Bake in a preheated oven at 200°C/400°F/ Gas Mark 6 for 20 minutes. Serve hot.

# Creamy Pasta & Broccoli

This colourful dish provides a mouthwatering contrast in the crisp al dente texture of the broccoli and the creamy cheese sauce.

## NUTRITIONAL INFORMATION

| | | |
|---|---|---|
| Calories .......472 | Sugars .........6g | |
| Protein ........15g | Fat ..........24g | |
| Carbohydrate ...52g | Saturates ......14g | |

  5 MINS    25 MINS

### SERVES 4

## INGREDIENTS

60 g/2 oz/4 tbsp butter

1 large onion, finely chopped

450 g/1 lb dried ribbon pasta

450 g/1 lb broccoli,
  broken into florets

150 ml/¼ pint/⅔ cup boiling
  vegetable stock

1 tbsp plain (all-purpose) flour

150 ml/¼ pint/⅔ cup single (light) cream

60 g/2 oz/½ cup grated mozzarella cheese

freshly grated nutmeg

salt and white pepper

fresh apple slices, to garnish

1 Melt half of the butter in a large saucepan over a medium heat. Add the onion and fry for 4 minutes.

## VARIATION

This dish would also be delicious and look just as colourful made with Cape broccoli, which is actually a purple variety of cauliflower and not broccoli at all.

2 Add the broccoli and pasta to the pan and cook, stirring constantly, for 2 minutes. Add the vegetable stock, bring back to the boil and simmer for a further 12 minutes. Season well with salt and white pepper.

3 Meanwhile, melt the remaining butter in a saucepan over a medium heat. Sprinkle over the flour and cook, stirring constantly, for 2 minutes. Gradually stir in the cream and bring to simmering point, but do not boil. Add the grated cheese and season with salt and a little freshly grated nutmeg.

4 Drain the pasta and broccoli mixture and pour over the cheese sauce. Cook, stirring occasionally, for about 2 minutes. Transfer the pasta and broccoli mixture to a warm, large, deep serving dish and serve garnished with slices of fresh apple.

# Vegetable Pasta Nests

These large pasta nests look impressive when presented filled with grilled (broiled) mixed vegetables, and taste delicious.

## NUTRITIONAL INFORMATION

| | | |
|---|---|---|
| Calories .......392 | Sugars .........1g | |
| Protein .........6g | Fat ..........28g | |
| Carbohydrate ...32g | Saturates .......9g | |

 25 MINS    40 MINS

### SERVES 4

## I N G R E D I E N T S

175 g/6 oz spaghetti

1 aubergine (eggplant), halved and sliced

1 courgette (zucchini), diced

1 red (bell) pepper, seeded and chopped
   diagonally

6 tbsp olive oil

2 garlic cloves, crushed

50 g/1¾ oz/4 tbsp butter or margarine,
   melted

15 g/½ oz/1 tbsp dry white breadcrumbs

salt and pepper

fresh parsley sprigs, to garnish

1 Bring a large saucepan of water to the boil and cook the spaghetti for 8–10 minutes or until al dente. Drain the spaghetti in a colander and set aside until required.

2 Place the aubergine (eggplant), courgette (zucchini) and (bell) pepper on a baking tray (cookie sheet).

3 Mix the oil and garlic together and pour over the vegetables, tossing to coat all over.

4 Cook under a preheated hot grill (broiler) for about 10 minutes,

turning, until tender and lightly charred. Set aside and keep warm.

5 Divide the spaghetti among 4 lightly greased Yorkshire pudding tins (pans). Using 2 forks, curl the spaghetti to form nests.

6 Brush the pasta nests with melted butter or margarine and sprinkle with the breadcrumbs. Bake in a preheated oven, at 200°C/400°F/ Gas Mark 6, for 15 minutes or until lightly golden. Remove the pasta nests from the tins (pans) and

transfer to serving plates. Divide the grilled (broiled) vegetables between the pasta nests, season and garnish.

### COOK'S TIP

'Al dente' means 'to the bite' and describes cooked pasta that is not too soft, but still has a 'bite' to it.

# Vermicelli & Vegetable Flan

Lightly cooked vermicelli is pressed into a flan ring and baked with a creamy mushroom filling.

    15 MINS   🕐 1 HOUR

### SERVES 4

## INGREDIENTS

75 g/2¾ oz/6 tbsp butter, plus extra
   for greasing

225 g/8 oz dried vermicelli or spaghetti

1 tbsp olive oil

1 onion, chopped

140 g/5 oz button mushrooms

1 green (bell) pepper, cored, seeded and
   sliced into thin rings

150 ml/¼ pint/⅔ cup milk

3 eggs, lightly beaten

2 tbsp double (heavy) cream

1 tsp dried oregano

freshly grated nutmeg

1 tbsp freshly grated Parmesan cheese

salt and pepper

tomato and basil salad, to serve

1 Generously grease a 20 cm/8 inch loose-based flan tin (pan) with butter.

2 Bring a large pan of lightly salted water to the boil. Add the vermicelli and olive oil and cook for 8–10 minutes until tender, but still firm to the bite. Drain, return to the pan, add 25 g/1 oz/ 2 tbsp of the butter and shake the pan to coat the pasta.

3 Press the pasta on to the base and around the sides of the flan tin (pan) to make a flan case.

4 Melt the remaining butter in a frying pan (skillet) over a medium heat. Add the onion and fry until it is translucent.

5 Add the mushrooms and (bell) pepper rings to the frying pan (skillet) and cook, stirring, for 2–3 minutes. Spoon the onion, mushroom and (bell) pepper mixture into the flan case and press it evenly into the base.

6 Beat together the milk, eggs and cream, stir in the oregano and season to taste with nutmeg and pepper. Carefully pour this mixture over the vegetables and then sprinkle with the Parmesan cheese.

7 Bake the flan in a preheated oven at 180°C/350°F/Gas Mark 4 for 40–45 minutes, or until the filling has set.

8 Slide the flan out of the tin (pan) and serve warm with a tomato and basil salad, if wished.

# Vegetable Lasagne

This rich, baked pasta dish is packed full of vegetables, tomatoes and Italian mozzarella cheese.

## NUTRITIONAL INFORMATION

Calories . . . . . . . .510   Sugars . . . . . . . .14g
Protein . . . . . . . .17g   Fat . . . . . . . . . .38g
Carbohydrate . . .28g   Saturates . . . . . .14g

50 MINS        50 MINS

### SERVES 6

## INGREDIENTS

1 kg/2 lb 4 oz aubergines (eggplant)

8 tbsp olive oil

25 g/1/oz/2 tbsp garlic and herb butter

450 g/1 lb courgettes (zucchini), sliced

225 g/8 oz/2 cups grated
   mozzarella cheese

600 ml/1 pint/2½ cups passata (sieved
   tomatoes)

6 sheets pre-cooked green lasagne

600 ml/1 pint/2½ cups béchamel sauce

60 g/2 oz/⅔ cup freshly grated
   Parmesan cheese

1 tsp dried oregano

salt and pepper

1 Thinly slice the aubergines (eggplant) and place in a colander. Sprinkle with salt and set aside for 20 minutes. Rinse and pat dry with kitchen paper.

2 Heat 4 tablespoons of the oil in a large frying pan (skillet). Fry half of the aubergine (eggplant) slices over a low heat for 6–7 minutes, or until golden. Drain thoroughly on kitchen paper. Repeat with the remaining oil and aubergine (eggplant) slices.

3 Melt the garlic and herb butter in the frying pan (skillet). Add the courgettes (zucchini) and fry for 5–6 minutes, until golden brown all over. Drain thoroughly on kitchen paper.

4 Place half of the aubergine (eggplant) and courgette (zucchini) slices in a large ovenproof dish. Season with pepper and sprinkle over half of the mozzarella cheese. Spoon over half of the passata

(sieved tomatoes) and top with 3 sheets of lasagne. Repeat the process, ending with a layer of lasagne.

5 Spoon over the béchamel sauce and sprinkle over the Parmesan cheese and oregano. Put the dish on a baking tray (cookie sheet) and bake in a preheated oven, at 220°C/425°F/Gas Mark 7, for 30–35 minutes, or until golden brown. Serve immediately.

# Gnocchi with Herb Sauce

These little potato dumplings are a traditional Italian appetizer but, served with a salad and bread, they make a substantial main course.

## NUTRITIONAL INFORMATION

| | | |
|---|---|---|
| Calories . . . . . . . .619 | Sugars . . . . . . . . .3g | |
| Protein . . . . . . . .11g | Fat . . . . . . . . .30g | |
| Carbohydrate . . .81g | Saturates . . . . . . .9g | |

🍲 30 MINS   🕐 30 MINS

### SERVES 6

## I N G R E D I E N T S

1 kg/2 lb 4 oz old potatoes, cut into
   1 cm/½ inch pieces

60 g/2 oz/¼ cup butter or margarine

1 egg, beaten

300 g/10½ oz/2½ cups plain
   (all-purpose) flour

salt

### S A U C E

125 ml/4 fl oz/½ cup olive oil

2 garlic cloves, very finely chopped

1 tbsp chopped fresh oregano

1 tbsp chopped fresh basil

salt and pepper

### T O   S E R V E

freshly grated Parmesan (optional)

mixed salad (greens)

warm ciabatta

**1** Cook the potatoes in a saucepan of boiling salted water for about 10 minutes or until tender. Drain well.

**2** Press the hot potatoes through a sieve (strainer) into a large bowl. Add 1 teaspoon of salt, the butter or margarine, egg and 150 g/5½ oz/1¼ cups of the flour. Mix well to bind together.

**3** Turn on to a lightly floured surface and knead, gradually adding the remaining flour, until a smooth, soft, slightly sticky dough is formed.

**4** Flour the hands and roll the dough into 2 cm/¾ inch thick rolls. Cut into 1 cm/½ inch pieces. Press the top of each piece with the floured prongs of a fork and spread out on a floured tea towel (dish cloth).

**5** Bring a large saucepan of salted water to a simmer. Add the gnocchi and cook in batches for 2–3 minutes or until they rise to the surface.

**6** Remove the gnocchi with a perforated spoon and put in a warmed, greased serving dish. Cover and keep warm.

**7** To make the sauce, put the oil, garlic and seasoning in a pan and cook, stirring, for 3–4 minutes until the garlic is golden. Remove from the heat and stir in the herbs. Pour over the gnocchi and serve, sprinkled with Parmesan, and accompanied by salad and warm ciabatta.

# Patriotic Pasta

The ingredients of this dish have the same bright colours as the Italian flag – hence its name.

## NUTRITIONAL INFORMATION

| | | |
|---|---|---|
| Calories .......325 | Sugars .........5g | |
| Protein .........8g | Fat ..........13g | |
| Carbohydrate ...48g | Saturates .......2g | |

 5 MINS     15 MINS

### SERVES 4

## INGREDIENTS

450 g/1 lb/4 cups dried farfalle

4 tbsp olive oil

450 g/1 lb cherry tomatoes

90 g/3 oz rocket (arugula)

salt and pepper

Pecorino cheese, to garnish

1 Bring a large saucepan of lightly salted water to the boil. Add the farfalle and 1 tablespoon of the olive oil and cook for 8–10 minutes or until tender, but still firm to the bite. Drain the farfalle thoroughly and return to the pan.

2 Cut the cherry tomatoes in half and trim the rocket (arugula).

### COOK'S TIP

Pecorino cheese is a hard sheep's milk cheese which resembles Parmesan and is often used for grating over a variety of dishes. It has a sharp flavour and is only used in small quantities.

3 Heat the remaining olive oil in a large saucepan. Add the tomatoes to the pan and cook for 1 minute. Add the farfalle and the rocket (arugula) to the pan and stir gently to mix. Heat through and then season to taste with salt and pepper.

4 Meanwhile, using a vegetable peeler, shave thin slices of Pecorino cheese.

5 Transfer the farfalle and vegetables to a warm serving dish. Garnish with the Pecorino cheese shavings and serve immediately.

# Spaghetti & Mushroom Sauce

This easy-to-cook dish is ideal for busy people with little time, but good taste!

## NUTRITIONAL INFORMATION

| | | | |
|---|---|---|---|
| Calories | .......604 | Sugars | .........5g |
| Protein | ........11g | Fat | ..........39g |
| Carbohydrate | ...54g | Saturates | ......21g |

20 MINS    35 MINS

### SERVES 4

## I N G R E D I E N T S

60 g/2 oz/4 tbsp butter

2 tbsp olive oil

6 shallots, sliced

450 g/1 lb/6 cups sliced button mushrooms

1 tsp plain (all-purpose) flour

150 ml/¼ pint/⅔ cup double (heavy) cream

2 tbsp port

115 g/4 oz sun-dried tomatoes, chopped

freshly grated nutmeg

450g /1 lb dried spaghetti

1 tbsp freshly chopped parsley

salt and pepper

6 triangles of fried white bread, to serve

1 Heat the butter and 1 tbsp of the oil in a large pan. Add the shallots and cook over a medium heat for 3 minutes. Add the mushrooms and cook over a low heat for 2 minutes. Season with salt and pepper, sprinkle over the flour and cook, stirring constantly, for 1 minute.

2 Gradually stir in the cream and port, add the sun-dried tomatoes and a pinch of grated nutmeg and cook over a low heat for 8 minutes.

3 Meanwhile, bring a large saucepan of lightly salted water to the boil.

Add the spaghetti and remaining olive oil and cook for 12–14 minutes, until tender but still firm to the bite.

4 Drain the spaghetti and return to the pan. Pour over the mushroom sauce and cook for 3 minutes. Transfer the spaghetti and mushroom sauce to a large serving plate and sprinkle over the chopped parsley. Serve with crispy triangles of fried bread.

## VARIATION

Non-vegetarians could add 115 g/4 oz Parma ham (prosciutto), cut into thin strips and heated gently in 25 g/1 oz/ 2 tbsp butter, to the pasta along with the mushroom sauce.

# Macaroni & Corn Pancakes

This vegetable pancake can be filled with your favourite vegetables – a favourite alternative is shredded parsnips with 1 tbsp mustard.

## NUTRITIONAL INFORMATION

| | | |
|---|---|---|
| Calories . . . . . . . .702 | Sugars . . . . . . . . .4g |
| Protein . . . . . . . .13g | Fat . . . . . . . . . .50g |
| Carbohydrate . . .55g | Saturates . . . . . .23g |

15 MINS     40 MINS

### SERVES 4

## I N G R E D I E N T S

2 corn cobs

60 g/2 oz/4 tbsp butter

115 g/4 oz red (bell) peppers, cored, seeded and finely diced

285 g/10 oz/2½ cups dried short-cut macaroni

150 ml/¼ pint/⅔ cup double (heavy) cream

25 g/1 oz/¼ cup plain (all-purpose) flour

4 egg yolks

4 tbsp olive oil

salt and pepper

### T O  S E R V E

oyster mushrooms

fried leeks

1 Bring a saucepan of water to the boil, add the corn cobs and cook for about 8 minutes. Drain thoroughly and refresh under cold running water for 3 minutes. Carefully cut away the kernels on to kitchen paper (towels) and set aside to dry.

2 Melt 25 g/1 oz/2 tbsp of the butter in a frying pan (skillet). Add the (bell) peppers and cook over a low heat for 4 minutes. Drain and pat dry with kitchen paper (towels).

3 Bring a large saucepan of lightly salted water to the boil. Add the macaroni and cook for about 12 minutes, or until tender but still firm to the bite. Drain the macaroni thoroughly and leave to cool in cold water until required.

4 Beat together the cream, flour, a pinch of salt and the egg yolks in a bowl until smooth. Add the corn and (bell) peppers to the cream and egg mixture. Drain the macaroni and then toss into the corn and cream mixture. Season with pepper to taste.

5 Heat the remaining butter with the oil in a large frying pan (skillet). Drop spoonfuls of the mixture into the pan and press down until the mixture forms a flat pancake. Fry until golden on both sides, and all the mixture is used up. Serve immediately with oyster mushrooms and fried leeks.

# Spinach Gnocchi

These gnocchi or small dumplings are made with potato and flavoured with spinach and nutmeg and served in a tomato and basil sauce.

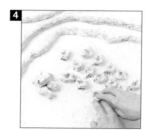
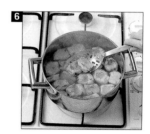

## NUTRITIONAL INFORMATION

Calories .......337  Sugars .........4g
Protein .........9g  Fat .........10g
Carbohydrate ...52g  Saturates .......4g

 25 MINS     1 HOUR

### SERVES 4

## I N G R E D I E N T S

450 g/1 lb baking potatoes

75 g/2¾ oz spinach

1 tsp water

25 g/1 oz/3 tbsp butter or margarine

1 small egg, beaten

150 g/5½ oz/¾ cup plain (all-purpose) flour

fresh basil sprigs, to garnish

### T O M A T O   S A U C E

1 tbsp olive oil

1 shallot, chopped

1 tbsp tomato purée (paste)

225 g/8 oz can chopped tomatoes

2 tbsp chopped basil

85 ml/3 fl oz/6 tbsp red wine

1 tsp caster (superfine) sugar

salt and pepper

1 Cook the potatoes in their skins in a pan of boiling salted water for 20 minutes. Drain well and press through a sieve into a bowl.

2 Cook the spinach in 1 teaspoon of water for 5 minutes or until wilted. Drain and pat dry with paper towels. Chop and stir into the potatoes.

3 Add the butter or margarine, egg and half of the flour to the spinach mixture, mixing well. Turn out on to a floured surface, gradually kneading in the remaining flour to form a soft dough.

4 With floured hands, roll the dough into thin ropes and cut off 2 cm/¾ inch pieces. Press the centre of each dumpling with your finger, drawing it towards you to curl the sides of the gnocchi. Cover the gnocchi and leave to chill.

5 Heat the oil for the sauce in a pan and sauté the chopped shallots for 5 minutes. Add the tomato purée (paste), tomatoes, basil, red wine and sugar and season well. Bring to the boil and then simmer for 20 minutes.

6 Bring a pan of salted water to the boil and cook the gnocchi for 2–3 minutes or until they rise to the top of the pan. Drain well and transfer to serving dishes. Spoon the tomato sauce over the gnocchi. Garnish and serve.

# Fettuccine & Walnut Sauce

This mouthwatering dish would make an excellent light, vegetarian lunch for four or a good starter for six.

## NUTRITIONAL INFORMATION

| | | | |
|---|---|---|---|
| Calories | .......833 | Sugars | .........5g |
| Protein | ........20g | Fat | ..........66g |
| Carbohydrate | ...44g | Saturates | ......15g |

15 MINS    10 MINS

### SERVES 6

## INGREDIENTS

2 thick slices wholemeal (whole-wheat)
  bread, crusts removed

300 ml/½ pint/1¼ cups milk

275 g/9½ oz/2½ cups shelled walnuts

2 garlic cloves, crushed

115 g/4 oz/1 cup stoned (pitted)
  black olives

60 g/2 oz/⅔ cup freshly grated
  Parmesan cheese

8 tbsp extra virgin olive oil

150 ml/¼ pint/⅔ cup double (heavy) cream

450 g/1 lb fresh fettuccine

salt and pepper

2–3 tbsp chopped fresh parsley

1 Put the bread in a shallow dish, pour over the milk and set aside to soak until the liquid has been absorbed.

2 Spread the walnuts out on a baking tray (cookie sheet) and toast in a preheated oven, at 190°C/375°F/Gas Mark 5, for about 5 minutes, or until golden. Set aside to cool.

3 Put the soaked bread, walnuts, garlic, olives, Parmesan cheese and 6 tablespoons of the olive oil in a food processor and work to make a purée. Season to taste with salt and pepper and stir in the cream.

4 Bring a large pan of lightly salted water to the boil. Add the fettuccine and 1 tablespoon of the remaining oil and cook for 2–3 minutes, or until tender but still firm to the bite. Drain the fettuccine thoroughly and toss with the remaining olive oil.

5 Divide the fettuccine between individual serving plates and spoon the olive, garlic and walnut sauce on top. Sprinkle over the fresh parsley and serve.

## COOK'S TIP

Parmesan quickly loses its pungency and 'bite'. It is better to buy small quantities and grate it yourself. Wrapped in foil, it will keep in the refrigerator for several months.

# Italian Spaghetti

Delicious vegetables, cooked in a rich tomato sauce, make an ideal topping for nutty wholemeal (whole-wheat) pasta.

## NUTRITIONAL INFORMATION

Calories . . . . . . . .381    Sugars . . . . . . . . .9g
Protein . . . . . . . .11g    Fat . . . . . . . . . .16g
Carbohydrate . . .53g    Saturates . . . . . . .5g

20 MINS          35 MINS

### SERVES 4

## I N G R E D I E N T S

2 tbsp olive oil

1 large red onion, chopped

2 garlic cloves, crushed

1 tbsp lemon juice

4 baby aubergines (eggplant), quartered

600 ml/1 pint/2½ cups passata
(sieved tomatoes)

2 tsp caster (superfine) sugar

2 tbsp tomato purée (paste)

400 g/14 oz can artichoke hearts, drained
and halved

115 g/4 oz/1 cup stoned (pitted)
black olives

350 g/12 oz dried spaghetti

25 g/1 oz/2 tbsp butter

salt and pepper

fresh basil sprigs, to garnish

olive bread, to serve

1 Heat 1 tablespoon of the olive oil in a large frying pan (skillet). Add the onion, garlic, lemon juice and aubergines (eggplant) and cook over a low heat for 4–5 minutes, or until the onion and aubergines (eggplant) are lightly golden brown.

2 Pour in the passata (sieved tomatoes), season to taste with salt and pepper and stir in the caster (superfine) sugar and tomato purée (paste). Bring to the boil, lower the heat and then simmer, stirring occasionally, for 20 minutes.

3 Gently stir in the artichoke hearts and black olives and cook for 5 minutes.

4 Meanwhile, bring a large saucepan of lightly salted water to the boil. Add the spaghetti and the remaining oil and cook for 7–8 minutes, or until tender but still firm to the bite.

5 Drain the spaghetti thoroughly and toss with the butter. Transfer the spaghetti to a large serving dish.

6 Pour the vegetable sauce over the spaghetti, garnish with the sprigs of fresh basil and serve immediately with olive bread.

# Spinach & Mushroom Lasagne

Always check the seasoning of vegetables – you can always add a little more to a recipe, but you cannot take it out once it has been added.

## NUTRITIONAL INFORMATION

| | | |
|---|---|---|
| Calories .......720 | Sugars .........9g | |
| Protein ........31g | Fat ..........52g | |
| Carbohydrate ...36g | Saturates .....32g | |

  20 MINS    40 MINS

### SERVES 4

## INGREDIENTS

115 g/4 oz/8 tbsp butter, plus extra

  for greasing

2 garlic cloves, finely chopped

115 g/4 oz shallots

225 g/8 oz wild mushrooms,

  such as chanterelles

450 g/1 lb spinach, cooked, drained and

  finely chopped

225 g/8 oz/2 cups grated Cheddar cheese

¼ tsp freshly grated nutmeg

1 tsp chopped fresh basil

60 g/2 oz plain (all-purpose) flour

600 ml/1 pint/2½ cups hot milk

60 g/2 oz/ ⅔ cup grated Cheshire cheese

salt and pepper

8 sheets pre-cooked lasagne

## VARIATION

You could substitute 4 (bell) peppers for the spinach. Roast in a preheated oven, at 200°C/400°F/Gas Mark 6, for 20 minutes. Rub off the skins under cold water, deseed and chop before using.

1 Lightly grease a large ovenproof dish with a little butter.

2 Melt 60 g/2 oz/4 tbsp of the butter in a saucepan. Add the garlic, shallots and wild mushrooms and fry over a low heat for 3 minutes. Stir in the spinach, Cheddar cheese, nutmeg and basil. Season with salt and pepper to taste and set aside.

3 Melt the remaining butter in another saucepan over a low heat. Add the flour and cook, stirring constantly, for 1 minute. Gradually stir in the hot milk, whisking constantly until smooth. Stir in 25 g/1 oz/¼ cup of the Cheshire cheese and season to taste with salt and pepper.

4 Spread half of the mushroom and spinach mixture over the base of the prepared dish. Cover with a layer of lasagne and then with half of the cheese sauce. Repeat the process and sprinkle over the remaining Cheshire cheese.

5 Bake in a preheated oven, at 200°C/400°F/Gas Mark 6, for 30 minutes, or until golden brown. Serve hot.

# Pasta & Vegetable Sauce

The different shapes and textures of the vegetables make a mouthwatering presentation in this light and summery dish.

## NUTRITIONAL INFORMATION

| | | |
|---|---|---|
| Calories . . . . . . .389 | Sugars . . . . . . . . .4g | |
| Protein . . . . . . . .16g | Fat . . . . . . . . . .20g | |
| Carbohydrate . . .38g | Saturates . . . . . .11g | |

 10 MINS    30 MINS

### SERVES 4

## INGREDIENTS

225 g/8 oz/2 cups dried gemelli or other
  pasta shapes

1 tbsp olive oil

1 head green broccoli, cut into florets

2 courgettes (zucchini), sliced

225 g/8 oz asparagus spears

115 g/4 oz mangetout (snow peas)

115 g/4 oz frozen peas

25 g/1 oz/2 tbsp butter

3 tbsp vegetable stock

4 tbsp double (heavy) cream

freshly grated nutmeg

2 tbsp chopped fresh parsley

2 tbsp freshly grated Parmesan cheese

salt and pepper

1 Bring a large saucepan of lightly salted water to the boil. Add the pasta and olive oil and cook for 8–10 minutes or until tender, but still firm to the bite. Drain the pasta, return to the pan, cover and keep warm.

2 Steam the broccoli, courgettes (zucchini), asparagus spears and mangetout (snow peas) over a pan of boiling salted water until they are just beginning to soften. Remove from the heat and refresh in cold water. Drain and set aside.

3 Bring a small pan of lightly salted water to the boil. Add the frozen peas and cook for 3 minutes. Drain the peas, refresh in cold water and then drain again. Set aside with the other vegetables.

4 Put the butter and vegetable stock in a pan over a medium heat. Add all of the vegetables, reserving a few of the asparagus spears, and toss carefully with a wooden spoon until they have heated through, taking care not to break them up.

5 Stir in the cream and heat through without bringing to the boil. Season to taste with salt, pepper and nutmeg.

6 Transfer the pasta to a warmed serving dish and stir in the chopped parsley. Spoon over the vegetable sauce and sprinkle over the Parmesan cheese. Arrange the reserved asparagus spears in a pattern on top and serve.

# Paglia e Fieno

The name of this dish – 'straw and hay' – refers to the colours of the pasta when mixed together.

## NUTRITIONAL INFORMATION

| | |
|---|---|
| Calories . . . . . . . .699 | Sugars . . . . . . . . .7g |
| Protein . . . . . . . .26g | Fat . . . . . . . . . .39g |
| Carbohydrate . . .65g | Saturates . . . . . .23g |

 10 MINS     10 MINS

### SERVES 4

I N G R E D I E N T S

60 g/2 oz/4 tbsp butter

450 g/1 lb fresh peas, shelled

200 ml/7 fl oz/ ⅞ cup double (heavy) cream

450 g/1 lb mixed fresh green and white
  spaghetti or tagliatelle

1 tbsp olive oil

60 g/2/ oz/⅔ cup freshly grated Parmesan
  cheese, plus extra to serve

pinch of freshly grated nutmeg

salt and pepper

1 Melt the butter in a large saucepan. Add the peas and cook, over a low heat, for 2–3 minutes.

2 Using a measuring jug (pitcher), pour 150 ml/¼ pint/⅔ cup of the cream into the pan, bring to the boil and simmer for 1–1½ minutes, or until slightly thickened. Remove the pan from the heat.

3 Meanwhile, bring a large pan of lightly salted water to the boil. Add the spaghetti or tagliatelle and olive oil and cook for 2–3 minutes, or until just tender but still firm to the bite. Remove the pan from the heat, drain the pasta thoroughly and return to the pan.

4 Add the peas and cream sauce to the pasta. Return the pan to the heat and add the remaining cream and the Parmesan cheese and season to taste with salt, pepper and grated nutmeg.

5 Using 2 forks, gently toss the pasta to coat with the peas and cream sauce, while heating through.

6 Transfer the pasta to a serving dish and serve immediately, with extra Parmesan cheese.

### VARIATION

Fry 140 g/5 oz/2 cups sliced button or oyster mushrooms in 60 g/2 oz/4 tbsp butter over a low heat for 4–5 minutes. Stir into the peas and cream sauce just before adding to the pasta in step 4.

# Green Tagliatelle with Garlic

A rich pasta dish for garlic lovers everywhere. It is quick and easy to prepare and full of flavour.

## NUTRITIONAL INFORMATION

Calories .......474   Sugars .........3g
Protein ........16g   Fat ..........24g
Carbohydrate ...52g   Saturates .......9g

 20 MINS    15 MINS

### SERVES 4

## INGREDIENTS

2 tbsp walnut oil

1 bunch spring onions (scallions), sliced

2 garlic cloves, thinly sliced

225 g/8 oz/3¼ cups sliced mushrooms

450 g/1 lb fresh green and white tagliatelle

1 tbsp olive oil

225 g/8 oz frozen spinach, thawed
    and drained

115 g/4 oz/½ cup full-fat soft cheese with
    garlic and herbs

4 tbsp single (light) cream

60 g/2 oz/½ cup chopped, unsalted
    pistachio nuts

salt and pepper

Italian bread, to serve

### TO GARNISH

2 tbsp shredded fresh basil

fresh basil sprigs

1 Heat the walnut oil in a large frying pan (skillet). Add the spring onions (scallions) and garlic and fry for 1 minute, until just softened.

2 Add the mushrooms to the pan, stir well, cover and cook over a low heat for about 5 minutes, until softened.

3 Meanwhile, bring a large saucepan of lightly salted water to the boil. Add the tagliatelle and olive oil and cook for 3–5 minutes, or until tender but still firm to the bite. Drain the tagliatelle thoroughly and return to the saucepan.

4 Add the spinach to the frying pan (skillet) and heat through for 1–2 minutes. Add the cheese to the pan and allow to melt slightly. Stir in the cream and cook, without allowing the mixture to come to the boil, until warmed through.

5 Pour the sauce over the pasta, season to taste with salt and pepper and mix well. Heat through gently, stirring constantly, for 2–3 minutes.

6 Transfer the pasta to a serving dish and sprinkle with the pistachio nuts and shredded basil. Garnish with the basil sprigs and serve immediately with the Italian bread of your choice.

# Spaghetti Olio e Aglio

This easy and satisfying Roman dish originated as a cheap meal for poor people, but has now become a favourite in restaurants and trattorias.

## NUTRITIONAL INFORMATION

| | |
|---|---|
| Calories . . . . . . . .515 | Sugars . . . . . . . . .1g |
| Protein . . . . . . . . .8g | Fat . . . . . . . . . .33g |
| Carbohydrate . . .50g | Saturates . . . . . . .5g |

5 MINS     5 MINS

### SERVES 4

## INGREDIENTS

125 ml/4 fl oz/½ cup olive oil

3 garlic cloves, crushed

450 g/1 lb fresh spaghetti

3 tbsp roughly chopped fresh parsley

salt and pepper

1 Reserve 1 tablespoon of the olive oil and heat the remainder in a medium saucepan. Add the garlic and a pinch of salt and cook over a low heat, stirring constantly, until golden brown, then remove the pan from the heat. Do not allow the garlic to burn as it will taint its flavour. (If it does burn, you will have to start all over again!)

2 Meanwhile, bring a large saucepan of lightly salted water to the boil. Add the spaghetti and remaining olive oil to the pan and cook for 2–3 minutes, or until tender, but still firm to the bite. Drain the spaghetti thoroughly and return to the pan.

3 Add the oil and garlic mixture to the spaghetti and toss to coat thoroughly. Season with pepper, add the chopped fresh parsley and toss to coat again.

4 Transfer the spaghetti to a warm serving dish and serve immediately.

## COOK'S TIP

Oils produced by different countries, mainly Italy, Spain and Greece, have their own characteristic flavours. Some produce an oil which has a hot, peppery taste while others have a 'green' flavour.

# Vegetables & Tofu

This is a simple, clean-tasting dish of green vegetables, tofu (bean curd) and pasta, lightly tossed in olive oil.

## NUTRITIONAL INFORMATION

Calories .......400  Sugars ........5g
Protein ........19g  Fat .........17g
Carbohydrate ...46g  Saturates ......5g

25 MINS     20 MINS

### SERVES 4

## INGREDIENTS

225 g/8 oz asparagus

125 g/4½ oz mangetout (snow peas)

225 g/8 oz French (green) beans

1 leek

225 g/8 oz shelled small broad (fava) beans

300 g/10½ oz dried fusilli

2 tbsp olive oil

25 g/1 oz/2 tbsp butter or margarine

1 garlic clove, crushed

225 g/8 oz tofu (bean curd), cut into
2.5 cm/1 inch cubes

60 g/2 oz/⅓ cup pitted green olives in
brine, drained

salt and pepper

freshly grated Parmesan, to serve

1 Cut the asparagus into 5 cm/2 inch lengths. Finely slice the mangetout (snow peas) diagonally and slice the French (green) beans into 2.5 cm/1 inch pieces. Finely slice the leek.

2 Bring a large saucepan of water to the boil and add the asparagus, green beans and broad (fava) beans. Bring back to the boil and cook for 4 minutes until just tender. Drain well and rinse in cold water. Set aside.

3 Bring a large saucepan of salted water to the boil and cook the fusilli for 8–9 minutes until just tender. Drain well. Toss in 1 tablespoon of the oil and season well.

4 Meanwhile, in a wok or large frying pan (skillet), heat the remaining oil and the butter or margarine and gently fry the leek, garlic and tofu (bean curd) for 1–2 minutes until the vegetables have just softened.

5 Stir in the mangetout (snow peas) and cook for 1 minute.

6 Add the boiled vegetables and olives to the pan and heat through for 1 minute. Carefully stir in the pasta and seasoning. Cook for 1 minute and pile into a warmed serving dish. Serve sprinkled with Parmesan.

# Pasta & Chilli Tomatoes

The pappardelle and vegetables are tossed in a delicious chilli and tomato sauce for a quick and economical meal.

## NUTRITIONAL INFORMATION

| | |
|---|---|
| Calories . . . . . . . .353 | Sugars . . . . . . . . .7g |
| Protein . . . . . . . .10g | Fat . . . . . . . . . .24g |
| Carbohydrate . . .26g | Saturates . . . . . . .4g |

 15 MINS  20 MINS

### SERVES 4

## I N G R E D I E N T S

275 g/9½ oz pappardelle

3 tbsp groundnut oil

2 cloves garlic, crushed

2 shallots, sliced

225 g/8 oz green beans, sliced

100 g/3½ oz cherry tomatoes, halved

1 tsp chilli flakes

4 tbsp crunchy peanut butter

150 ml/¼ pint/⅔ cup coconut milk

1 tbsp tomato purée (paste)

sliced spring onions (scallions), to garnish

1 Cook the pappardelle in a large saucepan of boiling, lightly salted water for 5-6 minutes.

## VARIATION

Non-vegetarians could add slices of chicken or beef to the recipe and stir-fry with the beans and pasta in step 5 for a more substantial main meal.

2 Heat the groundnut oil in a large pan or preheated wok.

3 Add the garlic and shallots and stir-fry for 1 minute.

4 Drain the pappardelle thoroughly and set aside.

5 Add the green beans and drained pasta to the wok and stir-fry for 5 minutes.

6 Add the cherry tomatoes to the wok and mix well.

7 Mix together the chilli flakes, peanut butter, coconut milk and tomato purée (paste).

8 Pour the chilli mixture over the noodles, toss well to combine and heat through.

9 Transfer to warm serving dishes and garnish. Serve immediately.

# Pasta with Nuts & Cheese

Simple and inexpensive, this tasty pasta dish can be prepared fairly quickly.

## NUTRITIONAL INFORMATION

| | | |
|---|---|---|
| Calories . . . . . . . .531 | Sugars . . . . . . . .4g | |
| Protein . . . . . . . .20g | Fat . . . . . . . . .35g | |
| Carbohydrate . . .35g | Saturates . . . . . .16g | |

10 MINS      30 MINS

### SERVES 4

## INGREDIENTS

60 g/2 oz/1 cup pine kernels (nuts)

350 g/12 oz dried pasta shapes

2 courgettes (zucchini), sliced

125 g/4½ oz/1¼ cups broccoli,
   broken into florets

200 g/7 oz/1 cup full-fat soft cheese

150 ml/¼ pint/⅔ cup milk

1 tbsp chopped fresh basil

125 g/4½ oz button mushrooms, sliced

90 g/3 oz blue cheese, crumbled

salt and pepper

sprigs of fresh basil, to garnish

green salad, to serve

1 Scatter the pine kernels (nuts) on to a baking tray (cookie sheet) and grill (broil), turning occasionally, until lightly browned all over. Set aside.

2 Cook the pasta in plenty of boiling salted water for 8–10 minutes or until just tender.

3 Meanwhile, cook the courgettes (zucchini) and broccoli in a small amount of boiling, lightly salted water for about 5 minutes or until just tender.

4 Put the soft cheese into a pan and heat gently, stirring constantly. Add the milk and stir to mix. Add the basil and mushrooms and cook gently for 2–3 minutes. Stir in the blue cheese and season to taste.

5 Drain the pasta and the vegetables and mix together. Pour over the cheese and mushroom sauce and add the pine kernels (nuts). Toss gently to mix. Garnish with basil sprigs and serve with a green salad.

# Pasta with Garlic & Broccoli

Broccoli coated in a garlic-flavoured cream sauce, served on herb tagliatelle. Try sprinkling with toasted pine nuts to add extra crunch.

## NUTRITIONAL INFORMATION

| | | | |
|---|---|---|---|
| Calories | .......538 | Sugars | .........4g |
| Protein | ........23g | Fat | ..........29g |
| Carbohydrate | ...50g | Saturates | ......17g |

 5 MINS    5 MINS

### SERVES 4

## I N G R E D I E N T S

500 g/1 lb 2 oz broccoli

300 g/10½ oz/1¼ cups garlic & herb cream cheese

4 tbsp milk

350 g/12 oz fresh herb tagliatelle

25 g/1 oz/¼ cup grated Parmesan cheese

chopped fresh chives, to garnish

1 Cut the broccoli into even-sized florets. Cook the broccoli in a saucepan of boiling salted water for 3 minutes and drain thoroughly.

2 Put the soft cheese into a saucepan and heat gently, stirring, until melted. Add the milk and stir until well combined.

3 Add the broccoli to the cheese mixture and stir to coat.

4 Meanwhile, bring a large saucepan of salted water to the boil and add the tagliatelle. Stir and bring back to the boil. Reduce the heat slightly and cook the tagliatelle, uncovered, for 3–4 minutes until just tender.

5 Drain the tagliatelle thoroughly and divide among 4 warmed serving plates. Spoon the broccoli and cheese sauce on top. Sprinkle with grated Parmesan cheese, garnish with chopped chives and serve.

## COOK'S TIP

A herb flavoured pasta goes particularly well with the broccoli sauce, but failing this, a tagliatelle verde or 'paglia e fieno' (literally 'straw and hay' – thin green and yellow noodles) will fit the bill.

# Basil & Tomato Pasta

Roasting the tomatoes gives a sweeter flavour to this sauce. Buy Italian tomatoes, such as plum or flavia, as these have a better flavour and colour.

## NUTRITIONAL INFORMATION

| | | |
|---|---|---|
| Calories .......177 | Sugars .........4g | |
| Protein .........5g | Fat ...........4g | |
| Carbohydrate ...31g | Saturates .......1g | |

 15 MINS    35 MINS

### SERVES 4

## INGREDIENTS

1 tbsp olive oil

2 sprigs rosemary

2 cloves garlic

450 g/1 lb tomatoes, halved

1 tbsp sun-dried tomato paste

12 fresh basil leaves, plus extra to garnish

salt and pepper

675 g/1½ lb fresh farfalle or 350 g/12 oz
   dried farfalle

1 Place the oil, rosemary, garlic and tomatoes, skin side up, in a shallow roasting tin (pan).

2 Drizzle with a little oil and cook under a preheated grill (broiler) for 20 minutes or until the tomato skins are slightly charred.

## COOK'S TIP

This sauce tastes just as good when served cold in a pasta salad.

3 Peel the skin from the tomatoes. Roughly chop the tomato flesh and place in a pan.

4 Squeeze the pulp from the garlic cloves and mix with the tomato flesh and sun-dried tomato paste.

5 Roughly tear the fresh basil leaves into smaller pieces and then stir them into the sauce. Season with a little salt and pepper to taste. Set aside.

6 Cook the farfalle in a saucepan of boiling water for 8–10 minutes or until it is cooked through, but still has 'bite'. Drain well.

7 Gently re-heat the tomato and basil sauce, stirring.

8 Transfer the farfalle to serving plates and pour over the basil and tomato sauce. Serve at once.

# Tagliatelle & Garlic Sauce

This pasta dish can be prepared in a moment – the intense flavours are sure to make this a popular recipe.

## NUTRITIONAL INFORMATION

Calories . . . . . . . .501   Sugars . . . . . . . . .3g
Protein . . . . . . . .15g    Fat . . . . . . . . . .31g
Carbohydrate . . .43g        Saturates . . . . . .11g

 15 MINS     20 MINS

### SERVES 4

## I N G R E D I E N T S

2 tbsp walnut oil

1 bunch spring onions (scallions), sliced

2 garlic cloves, sliced thinly

225 g/8 oz mushrooms, sliced

500 g/1 lb 2 oz fresh green and white
  tagliatelle

225 g/8 oz frozen chopped leaf spinach,
  thawed and drained

125 g/4½ oz/½ cup full-fat soft cheese with
  garlic and herbs

4 tbsp single (light) cream

60 g/2 oz/½ cup chopped, unsalted
  pistachio nuts

2 tbsp shredded fresh basil

salt and pepper

sprigs of fresh basil, to garnish

Italian bread, to serve

1 Gently heat the oil in a wok or frying pan (skillet) and fry the spring onions (scallions) and garlic for 1 minute or until just softened. Add the mushrooms, stir well, cover and cook gently for 5 minutes or until softened.

2 Meanwhile, bring a large saucepan of lightly salted water to the boil and cook the pasta for 3–5 minutes or until just tender. Drain the pasta thoroughly and return to the saucepan.

3 Add the spinach to the mushrooms and heat through for 1–2 minutes. Add the cheese and allow to melt slightly. Stir in the cream and continue to heat without allowing to boil.

4 Pour the mixture over the pasta, season to taste and mix well. Heat gently, stirring, for 2–3 minutes.

5 Pile into a warmed serving bowl and sprinkle over the pistachio nuts and shredded basil. Garnish with basil sprigs and serve with Italian bread.

# Potato & Spinach Gnocchi

These small potato dumplings are flavoured with spinach, cooked in boiling water and served with a simple tomato sauce.

## NUTRITIONAL INFORMATION

Calories . . . . . . . .315  Sugars . . . . . . . . .7g
Protein . . . . . . . . .8g  Fat . . . . . . . . . . .8g
Carbohydrate . . .56g  Saturates . . . . . . .1g

20 MINS        30 MINS

### SERVES 4

## I N G R E D I E N T S

300 g/10½ oz floury (mealy) potatoes, diced

175 g/6 oz spinach

1 egg yolk

1 tsp olive oil

125 g/4½ oz/1 cup plain (all-purpose) flour

salt and pepper

spinach leaves, to garnish

### S A U C E

1 tbsp olive oil

2 shallots, chopped

1 garlic clove, crushed

300 ml/½ pint/1¼ cups passata (sieved
tomatoes)

2 tsp soft light brown sugar

1 Cook the diced potatoes in a saucepan of boiling water for 10 minutes or until cooked through. Drain and mash the potatoes.

2 Meanwhile, in a separate pan, blanch the spinach in a little boiling water for 1-2 minutes. Drain the spinach and shred the leaves.

3 Transfer the mashed potato to a lightly floured chopping board and make a well in the centre. Add the egg yolk, olive oil, spinach and a little of the flour and quickly mix the ingredients into the potato, adding more flour as you go, until you have a firm dough. Divide the mixture into very small dumplings.

4 Cook the gnocchi, in batches, in a saucepan of boiling salted water for about 5 minutes or until they rise to the surface.

5 Meanwhile, make the sauce. Put the oil, shallots, garlic, passata (sieved tomatoes) and sugar into a saucepan and cook over a low heat for 10-15 minutes or until the sauce has thickened.

6 Drain the gnocchi using a perforated spoon and transfer to warm serving dishes. Spoon the sauce over the gnocchi and garnish with the fresh spinach leaves.

### VARIATION

Add chopped fresh herbs and cheese to the gnocchi dough instead of the spinach, if you prefer.

# Chilli & Pepper Pasta

This roasted (bell) pepper and chilli sauce is sweet and spicy – the perfect combination!

## NUTRITIONAL INFORMATION

| | | | |
|---|---|---|---|
| Calories | .......423 | Sugars | .........5g |
| Protein | .........9g | Fat | ..........27g |
| Carbohydrate | ...38g | Saturates | .......4g |

25 MINS    30 MINS

### SERVES 4

## INGREDIENTS

2 red (bell) peppers, halved and deseeded

1 small red chilli

4 tomatoes, halved

2 garlic cloves

50 g/1¾ oz ground almonds

7 tbsp olive oil

675 g/1½ lb fresh pasta or 350 g/12 oz
    dried pasta

fresh oregano leaves, to garnish

   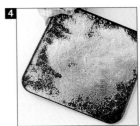

1 Place the (bell) peppers, skin-side up, on a baking tray (cookie sheet) with the chilli and tomatoes. Cook under a preheated grill (broiler) for 15 minutes or until charred. After 10 minutes turn the tomatoes skin-side up. Place the (bell) peppers and chillies in a polythene bag and leave to sweat for 10 minutes.

2 Remove the skin from the (bell) peppers and chillies and slice the flesh into strips, using a sharp knife.

3 Peel the garlic, and peel and deseed the tomatoes.

4 Place the almonds on a baking tray (cookie sheet) and place under the grill (broiler) for 2–3 minutes until golden.

5 Using a food processor, blend the (bell) pepper, chilli, garlic and tomatoes to make a purée. Keep the motor running and slowly add the olive oil to form a thick sauce. Alternatively, mash the mixture with a fork and beat in the olive oil, drop by drop.

6 Stir the toasted ground almonds into the mixture.

7 Warm the sauce in a saucepan until it is heated through.

8 Cook the pasta in a saucepan of boiling water for 8–10 minutes if using dried, or 3–5 minutes if using fresh. Drain the pasta thoroughly and transfer to a serving dish. Pour over the sauce and toss to mix. Garnish with the fresh oregano leaves.

## VARIATION

Add 2 tablespoons of red wine vinegar to the sauce and use as a dressing for a cold pasta salad, if you wish.

# Fettuccine all'Alfredo

This simple, traditional dish can be made with any long pasta, but is especially good with flat noodles, such as fettuccine or tagliatelle.

## NUTRITIONAL INFORMATION

Calories . . . . . . .627    Sugars . . . . . . . . .2g
Protein . . . . . . . .18g    Fat . . . . . . . . . .41g
Carbohydrate . . .51g    Saturates . . . . . .23g

 5 MINS     10 MINS

### SERVES 4

## I N G R E D I E N T S

25 g/1 oz/2 tbsp butter

200 ml/7 fl oz/⅞ cup double (heavy) cream

450 g/1 lb fresh fettuccine

1 tbsp olive oil

90 g/3 oz/1 cup freshly grated Parmesan
   cheese, plus extra to serve

pinch of freshly grated nutmeg

salt and pepper

fresh parsley sprigs, to garnish

1 Put the butter and 150 ml/
¼ pint/⅔ cup of the cream in a large saucepan and bring the mixture to the boil over a medium heat. Reduce the heat and then simmer gently for about 1½ minutes, or until slightly thickened.

2 Meanwhile, bring a large pan of lightly salted water to the boil. Add

## VARIATION

Traditionally, this classic Roman dish is served with the addition of strips of ham and fresh peas. Add 225 g/8 oz/2 cups shelled cooked peas and 175 g/6 oz ham strips with the Parmesan cheese in step 4.

the fettuccine and olive oil and cook for 2–3 minutes, until tender but still firm to the bite. Drain the fettuccine thoroughly and then pour over the cream sauce.

3 Toss the fettuccine in the sauce over a low heat until thoroughly coated.

4 Add the remaining cream, the Parmesan cheese and nutmeg to the fettuccine mixture and season to taste

with salt and pepper. Toss thoroughly to coat while gently heating through.

5 Transfer the fettuccine mixture to a warm serving plate and garnish with the fresh sprig of parsley. Serve immediately, with extra grated Parmesan cheese separately.

# Artichoke & Olive Spaghetti

The tasty flavours of artichoke hearts and black olives are a winning combination.

## NUTRITIONAL INFORMATION

| | | | |
|---|---|---|---|
| Calories | .......393 | Sugars | ........11g |
| Protein | ........14g | Fat | ...........11g |
| Carbohydrate | ...63g | Saturates | .......2g |

 20 MINS     35 MINS

### SERVES 4

### INGREDIENTS

2 tbsp olive oil

1 large red onion, chopped

2 garlic cloves, crushed

1 tbsp lemon juice

4 baby aubergines (eggplant), quartered

600 ml/1 pint/2½ cups passata (sieved tomatoes)

2 tsp caster (superfine) sugar

2 tbsp tomato purée (paste)

400 g/14 oz can artichoke hearts, drained and halved

125 g/4½ oz/¾ cup pitted black olives

350 g/12 oz wholewheat dried spaghetti

salt and pepper

sprigs of fresh basil, to garnish

olive bread, to serve

1 Heat 1 tablespoon of the oil in a large frying pan (skillet) and gently fry the onion, garlic, lemon juice and aubergines (eggplant) for 4–5 minutes or until lightly browned.

2 Pour in the passata (sieved tomatoes), season with salt and pepper to taste and add the sugar and tomato purée (paste). Bring to the boil, reduce the heat and simmer for 20 minutes.

3 Gently stir in the artichoke halves and olives and cook for 5 minutes.

4 Meanwhile, bring a large saucepan of lightly salted water to the boil, and cook the spaghetti for 8–10 minutes or until just tender. Drain well, toss in the remaining olive oil and season with salt and pepper to taste.

5 Transfer the spaghetti to a warmed serving bowl and top with the vegetable sauce. Garnish with basil sprigs and serve with olive bread.

# Spicy Tomato Tagliatelle

A deliciously fresh and slightly spicy tomato sauce which is excellent for lunch or a light supper.

## NUTRITIONAL INFORMATION

Calories .......306  Sugars .........7g
Protein .........8g  Fat ..........12g
Carbohydrate ...45g  Saturates .......7g

🥘 15 MINS  ⏱ 35 MINS

### SERVES 4

## I N G R E D I E N T S

50 g/1¾ oz/3 tbsp butter

1 onion, finely chopped

1 garlic clove, crushed

2 small red chillies,
   deseeded and diced

450 g/1 lb fresh tomatoes, skinned,
   deseeded and diced

200 ml/7 fl oz/¾ cup vegetable stock

2 tbsp tomato purée (paste)

1 tsp sugar

salt and pepper

675 g/1½ lb fresh green and white
   tagliatelle, or 350 g/12 oz dried

## VARIATION
Non-vegetarians could try topping this pasta dish with 50 g/1¾ oz pancetta or unsmoked bacon, diced and dry-fried for 5 minutes until crispy.

1 Melt the butter in a large saucepan. Add the onion and garlic and cook for 3–4 minutes or until softened.

2 Add the chillies to the pan and continue cooking for about 2 minutes.

3 Add the tomatoes and stock, reduce the heat and leave to simmer for 10 minutes, stirring.

4 Pour the sauce into a food processor and blend for 1 minute until smooth.

Alternatively, push the sauce through a sieve.

5 Return the sauce to the pan and add the tomato purée (paste) sugar, and salt and pepper to taste. Gently reheat over a low heat, until piping hot.

6 Cook the tagliatelle in a pan of boiling water for 8–10 minutes or until it is tender, but still has 'bite'. Drain the tagliatelle, transfer to serving plates and serve with the tomato sauce.

# Gnocchi Romana

This is a traditional Italian recipe but, for a less rich version, simply omit the eggs.

## NUTRITIONAL INFORMATION

Calories . . . . . . . .709   Sugars . . . . . . . . .9g
Protein . . . . . . . .32g   Fat . . . . . . . . . .41g
Carbohydrate . . .58g   Saturates . . . . . .25g

1¼ HOURS   45 MINS

### SERVES 4

## I N G R E D I E N T S

700 ml/1¼ pints/3⅛ cups milk

pinch of freshly grated nutmeg

90 g/3 oz/6 tbsp butter, plus extra
   for greasing

225 g/8 oz/1¼ cups semolina

125 g/4½ oz/1½ cups grated
   Parmesan cheese

2 eggs, beaten

60 g/2 oz/½ cup grated Gruyère (Swiss)
   cheese

salt and pepper

fresh basil sprigs, to garnish

1 Pour the milk into a pan and bring to
the boil. Remove the pan from the
heat and stir in the nutmeg, 25 g/
1 oz/2 tbsp of butter and salt and pepper.

2 Gradually stir the semolina into the
milk, whisking to prevent lumps
forming, and return the pan to a low heat.
Simmer, stirring constantly, for about
10 minutes, or until very thick.

3 Beat 60 g/2 oz/⅔ cup of Parmesan
cheese into the semolina mixture,
then beat in the eggs. Continue beating
the mixture until smooth. Set the mixture
aside for a few minutes to cool slightly.

4 Spread out the cooled semolina
mixture in an even layer on a sheet of
baking parchment or in a large, oiled
baking tin (pan), smoothing the surface
with a damp spatula – it should be 1 cm/
½ inch thick. Set aside to cool completely,
then chill in the refrigerator for 1 hour.

5 Once chilled, cut out rounds of
gnocchi, measuring about 4 cm/
1½ inches in diameter, using a plain,
greased pastry cutter.

6 Grease a shallow ovenproof dish or 4
individual dishes. Lay the gnocchi

trimmings in the base of the dish or dishes
and cover with overlapping rounds
of gnocchi.

7 Melt the remaining butter and drizzle
over the gnocchi. Sprinkle over the
remaining Parmesan cheese, then sprinkle
over the Gruyère (Swiss) cheese.

8 Bake in a preheated oven, at
200°C/400°F/Gas Mark 6, for 25–30
minutes, until the top is crisp and golden
brown. Serve hot, garnished with the basil.

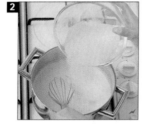 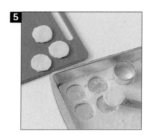 

# Pasta with Cheese & Broccoli

Some of the simplest and most satisfying dishes are made with pasta, such as this delicious combination of tagliatelle with two-cheese sauce.

## NUTRITIONAL INFORMATION

| Calories | .......624 | Sugars | .........2g |
|---|---|---|---|
| Protein | ........22g | Fat | ..........45g |
| Carbohydrate | ...34g | Saturates | ......28g |

 5 MINS     15 MINS

### SERVES 4

## I N G R E D I E N T S

300 g/10½ oz dried tagliatelle tricolore (plain, spinach- and tomato-flavoured noodles)

225 g/8 oz/2½ cups broccoli, broken into small florets

350g/12 oz/1½ cups Mascarpone cheese

125 g/4½ oz/1 cup blue cheese, chopped

1 tbsp chopped fresh oregano

25 g/1 oz/2 tbsp butter

salt and pepper

sprigs of fresh oregano, to garnish

freshly grated Parmesan, to serve

1 Cook the tagliatelle in plenty of boiling salted water for 8–10 minutes or until just tender.

2 Meanwhile, cook the broccoli florets in a small amount of lightly salted, boiling water. Avoid overcooking the broccoli, so that it retains much of its colour and texture.

3 Heat the Mascarpone and blue cheeses together gently in a large saucepan until they are melted. Stir in the oregano and season with salt and pepper to taste.

4 Drain the pasta thoroughly. Return it to the saucepan and add the butter, tossing the tagliatelle to coat it. Drain the broccoli well and add to the pasta with the sauce, tossing gently to mix.

5 Divide the pasta between 4 warmed serving plates. Garnish with sprigs of fresh oregano and serve with freshly grated Parmesan.

# Leek & Tomato Timbales

Angel-hair pasta, known as cappellini, is mixed with fried leeks, sun-dried tomatoes, fresh oregano and beaten eggs, and baked in ramekins.

## NUTRITIONAL INFORMATION

Calories . . . . . . . .331   Sugars . . . . . . . .10g
Protein . . . . . . . .10g   Fat . . . . . . . . . .21g
Carbohydrate . . .26g   Saturates . . . . . . .9g

5-10 MINS      50 MINS

### SERVES 4

I N G R E D I E N T S

90 g/3 oz angel-hair pasta (cappellini)

25 g/1 oz/2 tbsp butter

1 tbsp olive oil

1 large leek, sliced finely

60 g/2 oz/½ cup sun-dried tomatoes in oil,
    drained and chopped

1 tbsp chopped fresh oregano
    or 1 tsp dried oregano

2 eggs, beaten

100 ml/3½ fl oz/generous ⅓ cup
    single (light) cream

1 tbsp freshly grated Parmesan

salt and pepper

sprigs of oregano, to garnish

lettuce leaves, to serve

S A U C E

1 small onion, chopped finely

1 small garlic clove, crushed

350 g/12 oz tomatoes, peeled and chopped

1 tsp mixed dried Italian herbs

4 tbsp dry white wine

1 Cook the pasta in plenty of boiling salted water for about 3 minutes until al dente (just tender). Drain and rinse with cold water to cool quickly.

2 Meanwhile, heat the butter and oil in a frying pan (skillet). Gently fry the leek until softened, about 5–6 minutes. Add the sun-dried tomatoes and oregano, and cook for a further 2 minutes. Remove from the heat.

3 Add the leek mixture to the pasta. Stir in the beaten eggs, cream and Parmesan. Season with salt and pepper. Divide between 4 greased ramekin dishes or dariole moulds (molds).

4 Place the dishes in a roasting tin (pan) with enough warm water to come halfway up their sides. Bake in a preheated oven, 180°C/350°F/Gas Mark 4, for about 30 minutes, until set.

5 Meanwhile, make the tomato sauce. Fry the onion and garlic in the remaining butter and oil until softened. Add the tomatoes, herbs and wine. Cover and cook gently for about 20 minutes until pulpy. Blend in a food processor until smooth, or press through a sieve.

6 Run a knife or small spatula around the edge of the ramekins, then turn out the timbales on to 4 warm serving plates. Pour over a little sauce and garnish with oregano. Serve with the lettuce leaves.

# Basil & Pine Nut Pesto

Delicious stirred into pasta, soups and salad dressings, pesto is available in most supermarkets, but making your own gives a concentrated flavour.

## NUTRITIONAL INFORMATION

| | |
|---|---|
| Calories . . . . . . . .321 | Sugars . . . . . . . . .1g |
| Protein . . . . . . . .11g | Fat . . . . . . . . . .17g |
| Carbohydrate . . .32g | Saturates . . . . . . .4g |

 15 MINS       10 MINS

### SERVES 4

## INGREDIENTS

about 40 fresh basil leaves,
    washed and dried

3 garlic cloves, crushed

25 g/1 oz pine nuts

50 g/1¾ oz Parmesan cheese, finely grated

2–3 tbsp extra virgin olive oil

salt and pepper

675 g/1½ lb fresh pasta or
    350 g/12 oz dried pasta

1 Rinse the basil leaves and pat them dry with paper towels.

2 Put the basil leaves, garlic, pine nuts and grated Parmesan into a food processor and blend for about 30 seconds or until smooth. Alternatively, pound all of the ingredients by hand, using a mortar and pestle.

3 If you are using a food processor, keep the motor running and slowly add the olive oil. Alternatively, add the oil drop by drop while stirring briskly. Season with salt and pepper to taste.

4 Cook the pasta in a saucepan of boiling water allowing 3–4 minutes for fresh pasta or 8–10 minutes for dried, or until it is cooked through, but still has 'bite'. Drain the pasta thoroughly in a colander.

5 Transfer the pasta to a serving plate and serve with the pesto. Toss to mix well and serve hot.

### COOK'S TIP

You can store pesto in the refrigerator for about 4 weeks. Cover the surface of the pesto with olive oil before sealing the container or bottle, to prevent the basil from oxidising and turning black.

# Pasta with Green Vegetables

The different shapes and textures of the vegetables make a mouthwatering presentation in this light and summery dish.

## NUTRITIONAL INFORMATION

Calories . . . . . . . . .517    Sugars . . . . . . . . .5g
Protein . . . . . . . .17g    Fat . . . . . . . . . .32g
Carbohydrate . . .42g    Saturates . . . . . .18g

10 MINS        25 MINS

### SERVES 4

## INGREDIENTS

225 g/8 oz gemelli or other pasta shapes

1 tbsp olive oil

2 tbsp chopped fresh parsley

2 tbsp freshly grated Parmesan

salt and pepper

### SAUCE

1 head of green broccoli, cut into florets

2 courgettes (zucchini), sliced

225 g/8 oz asparagus spears, trimmed

125 g/4½ oz mangetout (snow peas),
   trimmed

125 g/4½ oz frozen peas

25 g/1 oz/2 tbsp butter

3 tbsp vegetable stock

5 tbsp double (heavy) cream

large pinch of freshly grated nutmeg

1 Cook the pasta in a large pan of salted boiling water, adding the olive oil, for 8–10 minutes or until tender. Drain the pasta in a colander, return to the pan, cover and keep warm.

2 Steam the broccoli, courgettes (zucchini), asparagus spears and mangetout (snow peas) over a pan of boiling, salted water until just beginning to soften. Remove from the heat and plunge into cold water to prevent further cooking. Drain and set aside.

3 Cook the peas in boiling, salted water for 3 minutes, then drain. Refresh in cold water and drain again.

4 Put the butter and vegetable stock in a pan over a medium heat. Add all of the vegetables except for the asparagus spears and toss carefully with a wooden spoon to heat through, taking care not to break them up. Stir in the cream, allow the sauce to heat through and season with salt, pepper and nutmeg.

5 Transfer the pasta to a warmed serving dish and stir in the chopped parsley. Spoon the sauce over, and sprinkle on the freshly grated Parmesan. Arrange the asparagus spears in a pattern on top. Serve hot.

# Three-Cheese Macaroni

Based on a traditional family favourite, this pasta bake has plenty of flavour. Serve with a crisp salad for a quick, tasty supper.

## NUTRITIONAL INFORMATION

| | | |
|---|---|---|
| Calories . . . . . . .672 | Sugars . . . . . . . .10g | |
| Protein . . . . . . . .31g | Fat . . . . . . . . . .44g | |
| Carbohydrate . . .40g | Saturates . . . . . .23g | |

30 MINS   45 MINS

### SERVES 4

## INGREDIENTS

600 ml/1 pint/2½ cups white sauce

225 g/8 oz/2 cups macaroni

1 egg, beaten

125 g/4½ oz/1 cup grated mature (sharp) Cheddar

1 tbsp wholegrain mustard

2 tbsp chopped fresh chives

4 tomatoes, sliced

125 g/4½ oz/1 cup grated red Leicester (brick) cheese

60 g/2 oz/½ cup grated blue cheese

2 tbsp sunflower seeds

salt and pepper

snipped fresh chives, to garnish

1 Make the white sauce, put into a bowl and cover with cling film (plastic wrap) to prevent a skin forming. Set aside.

2 Bring a saucepan of salted water to the boil and cook the macaroni for 8–10 minutes or until just tender. Drain well and place in an ovenproof dish.

3 Stir the beaten egg, Cheddar, mustard, chives and seasoning into the white sauce and spoon over the macaroni, making sure it is well covered. Top with a layer of sliced tomatoes.

4 Sprinkle over the red Leicester (brick) and blue cheeses, and sunflower seeds. Put on a baking tray (cookie sheet) and bake in a preheated oven, 190°C/375°F/Gas Mark 5, for 25–30 minutes or until bubbling and golden. Garnish with chives and serve immediately.

# Vegetable & Pasta Parcels

These small parcels are very easy to make and have the advantage of being filled with your favourite mixture of succulent mushrooms.

## NUTRITIONAL INFORMATION

Calories . . . . . . . .333   Sugars . . . . . . . . .1g
Protein . . . . . . . . .7g   Fat . . . . . . . . . .30g
Carbohydrate . . .10g   Saturates . . . . . .13g

🕒 20 MINS          🕐 20 MINS

### SERVES 4

## I N G R E D I E N T S

### FILLING

25 g/1 oz/3 tbsp butter or margarine

2 garlic cloves, crushed

1 small leek, chopped

2 celery sticks, chopped

200 g/7 oz/2⅓ cups open-cap
   mushrooms, chopped

1 egg, beaten

2 tbsp grated Parmesan cheese

salt and pepper

### RAVIOLI

4 sheets filo pastry

25 g/1 oz/3 tbsp margarine

oil, for deep-frying

1 To make the filling, melt the butter or margarine in a frying pan (skillet) and sauté the garlic and leek for 2–3 minutes until softened.

2 Add the celery and mushrooms and cook for a further 4–5 minutes until all of the vegetables are tender.

3 Turn off the heat and stir in the egg and grated Parmesan cheese. Season with salt and pepper to taste.

4 Lay the pastry sheets on a chopping board and cut each into nine squares.

5 Spoon a little of the filling into the centre half of the squares and brush the edges of the pastry with butter or margarine. Lay another square on top and seal the edges to make a parcel.

6 Heat the oil for deep-frying to 180°C/350°F or until a cube of bread browns in 30 seconds. Fry the ravioli, in batches, for 2–3 minutes or until golden brown. Remove from the oil with a slotted spoon and pat dry on absorbent paper towels. Transfer to a warm serving plate and serve.

# Baked Pasta

This pasta dish is baked in a pudding basin (bowl) and served cut into slices. It looks and tastes terrific and is great when you want to impress.

## NUTRITIONAL INFORMATION

| | | | |
|---|---|---|---|
| Calories | .......179 | Sugars | .........6g |
| Protein | .........8g | Fat | ..........10g |
| Carbohydrate | ...16g | Saturates | .......3g |

  10 MINS     1 HR 5 MINS

### SERVES 8

## I N G R E D I E N T S

100 g/3½ oz/1 cup dried pasta shapes, such as penne or casareccia

1 tbsp olive oil

1 leek, chopped

3 garlic cloves, crushed

1 green (bell) pepper, seeded and chopped

400 g/14 oz can chopped tomatoes

2 tbsp chopped, pitted black olives

2 eggs, beaten

1 tbsp chopped basil

### T O M A T O   S A U C E

1 tbsp olive oil

1 onion, chopped

225 g/8 oz can chopped tomatoes

1 tsp caster (superfine) sugar

2 tbsp tomato purée (paste)

150 ml/¼ pint/¾ cup vegetable stock

salt and pepper

1 Cook the pasta in a saucepan of boiling lightly salted water for 8 minutes. Drain thoroughly.

2 Meanwhile, heat the oil in a saucepan. Add the leek and garlic and sauté, stirring constantly, for 2 minutes. Add the (bell) pepper, tomatoes and olives and cook for a further 5 minutes.

3 Remove the pan from the heat and stir in the pasta, beaten eggs and basil. Season well, and spoon into a lightly greased 1 litre/2 pint/4 cup ovenproof pudding basin (ovenproof bowl).

4 Place the pudding basin (bowl) in a roasting tin (pan) and half-fill the tin (pan) with boiling water. Cover and cook in a preheated oven, 180°C/350°F/Gas Mark 6, for 40 minutes, until set.

5 To make the sauce, heat the oil in a pan and sauté the onion for 2 minutes. Add the remaining ingredients and cook for 10 minutes. Put the sauce in a food processor or blender and process until smooth. Return to a clean saucepan and heat through.

6 Turn the pasta out of the pudding basin (bowl) on to a warm plate. Slice and serve with the tomato sauce.

# Vegetable Cannelloni

This dish is made with prepared cannelloni tubes, but may also be made by rolling ready-bought lasagne sheets.

## NUTRITIONAL INFORMATION

| | |
|---|---|
| Calories .......594 | Sugars ........12g |
| Protein ........13g | Fat ..........38g |
| Carbohydrate ...52g | Saturates .......7g |

10 MINS    45 MINS

### SERVES 4

## I N G R E D I E N T S

1 aubergine (eggplant)

125 ml/4 fl oz/½ cup olive oil

225 g/8 oz spinach

2 garlic cloves, crushed

1 tsp ground cumin

75 g/2¾ oz/1 cup mushrooms, chopped

12 cannelloni tubes

salt and pepper

### T O M A T O   S A U C E

1 tbsp olive oil

1 onion, chopped

2 garlic cloves, crushed

2 x 400 g/14 oz cans chopped tomatoes

1 tsp caster (superfine) sugar

2 tbsp chopped basil

50 g/1¾ oz/½ cup sliced mozzarella

## COOK'S TIP

You can prepare the tomato sauce in advance and store it in the refrigerator for up to 24 hours.

1 Cut the aubergine (eggplant) into small dice.

2 Heat the oil in a frying pan (skillet). Add the aubergine (eggplant) and cook over a moderate heat, stirring frequently, for 2–3 minutes.

3 Add the spinach, garlic, cumin and mushrooms. Season and cook, stirring, for 2–3 minutes. Spoon the mixture into the cannelloni tubes and place in an ovenproof dish in a single layer.

4 To make the sauce, heat the olive oil in a saucepan and sauté the onion and garlic for 1 minute. Add the tomatoes, caster (superfine) sugar and chopped basil and bring to the boil. Reduce the heat and simmer for about 5 minutes. Pour the sauce over the cannelloni tubes.

5 Arrange the sliced mozzarella on top of the sauce and cook in a preheated oven, 190°C/375°F/Gas Mark 5, for 30 minutes, or until the cheese is bubbling and golden brown. Serve immediately.

# Pear & Walnut Pasta

This is quite an unusual combination of ingredients in a savoury dish, but is absolutely wonderful tossed into a fine pasta, such as spaghetti.

## NUTRITIONAL INFORMATION

Calories . . . . . . .508  Sugars . . . . . . . . .9g
Protein . . . . . . . .15g  Fat . . . . . . . . . .27g
Carbohydrate . . .50g  Saturates . . . . . .11g

 10 MINS   20 MINS

### SERVES 4

### INGREDIENTS

225 g/8 oz dried spaghetti

2 small ripe pears, peeled and sliced

150 ml/¼ pint/¾ cup vegetable stock

6 tbsp dry white wine

25 g/1 oz/2 tbsp butter

1 tbsp olive oil

1 red onion, quartered and sliced

1 garlic clove, crushed

50 g/1¾ oz/½ cup walnut halves

2 tbsp chopped oregano

1 tbsp lemon juice

75 g/2¾ oz dolcelatte cheese

salt and pepper

oregano sprigs, to garnish

1 Cook the pasta in a saucepan of boiling lightly salted water for about 8–10 minutes, or until al dente. Drain thoroughly and keep warm until required.

2 Meanwhile, place the pears in a pan and pour over the stock and wine. Poach the pears over a low heat for 10 minutes. Drain and reserve the cooking liquid and set the pears aside.

3 Heat the butter and oil in a saucepan until the butter melts. Add the onion and garlic and sauté over a low heat, stirring frequently for 2–3 minutes.

4 Stir in the walnut halves, oregano and lemon juice.

5 Stir in the reserved pears with 4 tablespoons of the poaching liquid.

6 Crumble the dolcelatte cheese into the pan and cook over a low heat, stirring occasionally, for 1–2 minutes, or until the cheese is just beginning to melt. Season with salt and pepper to taste.

7 Add the pasta and toss in the sauce, using two forks. Garnish and serve.

# Macaroni Cheese & Tomato

This is a really simple, family dish which is inexpensive and easy to prepare and cook. Serve with a salad or fresh green vegetables.

## NUTRITIONAL INFORMATION

Calories . . . . . . . .592    Sugars . . . . . . . . .6g
Protein . . . . . . . .28g    Fat . . . . . . . . . .29g
Carbohydrate . . .57g    Saturates . . . . . .17g

 15 MINS     35–40 MINS

### SERVES 4

## I N G R E D I E N T S

225 g/8 oz/2 cups dried elbow macaroni

175 g/6 oz/1½ cups grated Cheddar cheese

100 g/3½ oz/1 cup grated
  Parmesan cheese

4 tbsp fresh white breadcrumbs

1 tbsp chopped basil

1 tbsp butter or margarine, plus extra
  for greasing

### T O M A T O   S A U C E

1 tbsp olive oil

1 shallot, finely chopped

2 garlic cloves, crushed

500 g/1 lb 2 oz canned chopped tomatoes

1 tbsp chopped basil

salt and pepper

1 To make the tomato sauce, heat the oil in a heavy-based saucepan. Add the shallots and garlic and sauté for 1 minute. Add the tomatoes and basil and season with salt and pepper to taste. Cook over a medium heat, stirring constantly, for 10 minutes.

2 Meanwhile, cook the macaroni in a large pan of boiling lightly salted water for 8 minutes, or until al dente. Drain thoroughly and set aside.

3 Mix the Cheddar and Parmesan together in a bowl. Grease a deep, ovenproof dish. Spoon one-third of the tomato sauce into the base of the dish, top with one-third of the macaroni and then one-third of the cheeses. Season to taste with salt and pepper. Repeat these layers twice, ending with a layer of grated cheese.

4 Combine the breadcrumbs and basil and sprinkle evenly over the top. Dot the topping with the butter or margarine and cook in a preheated oven, 190°C/375°F/Gas Mark 5, for 25 minutes, or until the the topping is golden brown and bubbling. Serve immediately.

# Gnocchi & Tomato Sauce

Freshly made potato gnocchi are delicious, especially when they are topped with a fragrant tomato sauce.

## NUTRITIONAL INFORMATION

Calories . . . . . . . .216    Sugars . . . . . . . . .5g
Protein . . . . . . . . .5g    Fat . . . . . . . . . . .6g
Carbohydrate . . .39g    Saturates . . . . . . .1g

30 MINS          45 MINS

### SERVES 4

## INGREDIENTS

350 g/12 oz floury (mealy) potatoes (those
   suitable for baking or mashing), halved

75 g/2¾ oz self-raising flour, plus extra for
   rolling out

2 tsp dried oregano

2 tbsp oil

1 large onion, chopped

2 garlic cloves, chopped

400 g/14 oz can chopped tomatoes

½ vegetable stock cube dissolved in
   100 ml/3½ fl oz/⅓ cup boiling water

2 tbsp basil, shredded, plus whole

leaves to garnish

salt and pepper

Parmesan cheese, grated, to serve

1 Bring a large saucepan of water to the boil. Add the potatoes and cook for 12–15 minutes or until tender. Drain and leave to cool.

2 Peel and then mash the potatoes with the salt and pepper, sifted flour and oregano. Mix together with your hands to form a dough.

3 Heat the oil in a pan. Add the onions and garlic and cook for 3–4 minutes.

Add the tomatoes and stock and cook, uncovered, for 10 minutes. Season with salt and pepper to taste.

4 Roll the potato dough into a sausage about 2.5 cm/1 inch in diameter. Cut the sausage into 2.5 cm/1 inch lengths. Flour your hands, then press a fork into each piece to create a series of ridges on one side and the indent of your index finger on the other.

5 Bring a large saucepan of water to the boil and cook the gnocchi, in batches, for 2–3 minutes. They should rise to the surface when cooked. Drain well and keep warm.

6 Stir the basil into the tomato sauce and pour over the gnocchi. Garnish with basil leaves and season with pepper to taste. Sprinkle with Parmesan and serve at once.

## VARIATION

Try serving the gnocchi with pesto sauce for a change.

# Baked Sweet Ravioli

These scrumptious little parcels are the perfect dessert for anyone with a really sweet tooth.

## NUTRITIONAL INFORMATION

Calories .......765  Sugars ........56g
Protein ........16g  Fat ..........30g
Carbohydrate ...114g  Saturates ......15g

1½ HOURS     20 MINS

### SERVES 4

## INGREDIENTS

### PASTA

425 g/15 oz/3¾ cups plain

(all purpose) flour

140 g/5 oz/10 tbsp butter, plus extra

for greasing

140 g/5 oz/¾ cup caster (superfine) sugar

4 eggs

25 g/1 oz yeast

125 ml/4 fl oz warm milk

### FILLING

175 g/6 oz/⅔ cup chestnut purée (paste)

60 g/2 oz/½ cup cocoa powder

60 g/2 oz/¼ cup caster (superfine) sugar

60 g/2 oz/½ cup chopped almonds

60 g/2 oz/1 cup crushed amaretti

biscuits (cookies)

175 g/6 oz/⅝ cup orange marmalade

1 To make the sweet pasta dough, sift the flour into a mixing bowl, then mix in the butter, sugar and 3 eggs.

2 Mix together the yeast and warm milk in a small bowl and when thoroughly combined, mix into the dough.

3 Knead the dough for 20 minutes, cover with a clean cloth and set aside in a warm place for 1 hour to rise.

4 Mix together the chestnut purée (paste), cocoa powder, sugar, almonds, crushed amaretti biscuits (cookies) and orange marmalade in a separate bowl.

5 Grease a baking tray (cookie sheet) with butter.

6 Lightly flour the work surface (counter). Roll out the pasta dough into a thin sheet and cut into 5 cm/2 inch rounds with a plain pastry cutter.

7 Put a spoonful of filling on to each round and then fold in half, pressing the edges to seal. Arrange on the prepared baking tray (cookie sheet), spacing the ravioli out well.

8 Beat the remaining egg and brush all over the ravioli to glaze. Bake in a preheated oven, at 180°C/350°F/Gas Mark 4, for 20 minutes. Serve hot.

# Raspberry Fusilli

This is the ultimate in self-indulgence – a truly delicious dessert that tastes every bit as good as it looks.

## NUTRITIONAL INFORMATION

| | | | |
|---|---|---|---|
| Calories | .......235 | Sugars | ........20g |
| Protein | .........7g | Fat | ...........7g |
| Carbohydrate | ...36g | Saturates | .......1g |

5 MINS    20 MINS

### SERVES 4

## I N G R E D I E N T S

175 g/6 oz/½ cup fusilli

700 g/1 lb 9 oz/4 cups raspberries

2 tbsp caster (superfine) sugar

1 tbsp lemon juice

4 tbsp flaked (slivered) almonds

3 tbsp raspberry liqueur

1 Bring a large saucepan of lightly salted water to the boil. Add the fusilli and cook for 8–10 minutes until tender, but still firm to the bite. Drain the fusilli thoroughly, return to the pan and set aside to cool.

2 Using a spoon, firmly press 225 g/ 8 oz/1⅓ cups of the raspberries through a sieve (strainer) set over a large mixing bowl to form a smooth purée (paste).

3 Put the raspberry purée (paste) and sugar in a small saucepan and simmer over a low heat, stirring occasionally, for 5 minutes.

4 Stir in the lemon juice and set the sauce aside until required.

5 Add the remaining raspberries to the fusilli in the pan and mix together well. Transfer the raspberry and fusilli mixture to a serving dish.

6 Spread the almonds out on a baking tray (cookie sheet) and toast under the grill (broiler) until golden brown. Remove and set aside to cool slightly.

7 Stir the raspberry liqueur into the reserved raspberry sauce and mix together well until very smooth. Pour the raspberry sauce over the fusilli, sprinkle over the toasted almonds and serve.

## VARIATION

You could use any sweet, ripe berry for making this dessert. Strawberries and blackberries are especially suitable, combined with the correspondingly flavoured liqueur. Alternatively, you could use a different berry mixed with the fusilli, but still pour over raspberry sauce.

# Honey & Nut Nests

Pistachio nuts and honey are combined with crisp cooked angel hair pasta in this unusual dessert.

## NUTRITIONAL INFORMATION

| | | |
|---|---|---|
| Calories | . . . . . . .802 | Sugars . . . . . . . .53g |
| Protein | . . . . . . . .13g | Fat . . . . . . . . . .48g |
| Carbohydrate | . . .85g | Saturates . . . . . .16g |

 10 MINS      1 HOUR

## SERVES 4

## I N G R E D I E N T S

225 g/8 oz angel hair pasta

115 g/4 oz/8 tbsp butter

175 g/6 oz/1½ cups shelled pistachio nuts,
    chopped

115 g/4 oz/½ cup sugar

115 g/4 oz/⅓ cup clear honey

150 ml/¼ pint/⅔ cup water

2 tsp lemon juice

salt

Greek-style yogurt, to serve

1 Bring a large saucepan of lightly salted water to the boil. Add the angel hair pasta and cook for 8–10 minutes or until tender, but still firm to the bite. Drain the pasta and return to the pan. Add the butter and toss to coat the pasta thoroughly. Set aside to cool.

2 Arrange 4 small flan or poaching rings on a baking tray (cookie sheet). Divide the angel hair pasta into 8 equal quantities and spoon 4 of them into the rings. Press down lightly. Top the pasta with half of the nuts, then add the remaining pasta.

3 Bake in a preheated oven, at 180°C/350°F/Gas Mark 4, for 45 minutes, or until golden brown.

4 Meanwhile, put the sugar, honey and water in a saucepan and bring to the boil over a low heat, stirring constantly until the sugar has dissolved completely. Simmer for 10 minutes, add the lemon juice and simmer for 5 minutes.

5 Using a palette knife (spatula), carefully transfer the angel hair nests to a serving dish. Pour over the honey syrup, sprinkle over the remaining nuts and set aside to cool completely before serving. Serve the Greek-style yogurt separately.

## COOK'S TIP

Angel hair pasta is also known as *capelli d'Angelo*. Long and very fine, it is usually sold in small bunches that already resemble nests.

# German Noodle Pudding

This rich and satisfying pudding is a traditional Jewish recipe.

## NUTRITIONAL INFORMATION

| | | |
|---|---|---|
| Calories . . . . . . . .721 | Sugars . . . . . . . .27g | |
| Protein . . . . . . . .21g | Fat . . . . . . . . . .45g | |
| Carbohydrate . . .63g | Saturates . . . . . .24g | |

15 MINS        50 MINS

### SERVES 4

## I N G R E D I E N T S

0 g/2 oz/4 tbsp butter, plus extra for greasing

75 g/6 oz ribbon egg noodles

15 g/4 oz/½ cup cream cheese

25 g/8 oz/1 cup cottage cheese

0 g/3 oz/½ cup caster (superfine) sugar

eggs, lightly beaten

25 ml/4 fl oz/½ cup soured cream

tsp vanilla essence (extract)

pinch of ground cinnamon

tsp grated lemon rind

5 g/1 oz/¼ cup flaked (slivered) almonds

5 g/1 oz/⅜ cup dry white breadcrumbs

cing (confectioners') sugar, for dusting

## VARIATION

Although not authentic, you could add 3 tbsp raisins with the lemon rind in step 3, if liked.

1 Grease an ovenproof dish with butter.

2 Bring a large pan of water to the boil. Add the noodles and cook until almost tender. Drain and set aside.

3 Beat together the cream cheese, cottage cheese and caster (superfine) sugar in a mixing bowl. Beat in the eggs, a little at a time, until well combined. Stir in the soured cream, vanilla essence (extract), cinnamon and lemon rind, and fold in the noodles to coat. Transfer the mixture to the prepared dish and smooth the surface.

4 Melt the butter in a frying pan (skillet). Add the almonds and fry, stirring constantly, for about 1–1½ minutes, until lightly coloured. Remove the frying pan (skillet) from the heat and stir the breadcrumbs into the almonds.

5 Sprinkle the almond and breadcrumb mixture over the pudding and bake in a preheated oven at 180°C/350°F/Gas 4 for 35-40 minutes, until just set. Dust with a little icing (confectioners') sugar and serve immediately.

This is a Parragon Book
This edition published in 2003

Parragon
Queen Street House
4 Queen Street
Bath BA1 1HE, UK

ISBN: 1-40540-908-8

Printed in China

**NOTE**

This book uses metric and imperial measurements. Follow the same units
of measurement throughout; do not mix metric and imperial.
All spoon measurements are level: teaspoons are assumed to be 5 ml, and
tablespoons are assumed to be 15 ml. Unless otherwise stated,
milk is assumed to be full fat, eggs and individual vegetables such as potatoes
are medium, and pepper is freshly ground black pepper.

The nutritional information provided for each recipe is per serving or per person.
Optional ingredients, variations or serving suggestions have
not been included in the calculations. The times given for each recipe are an approximate
guide only because the preparation times may differ according to the techniques used by
different people and the cooking times may vary as a result of the type of oven used.

Recipes using raw or very lightly cooked eggs should be
avoided by infants, the elderly, pregnant women, convalescents,
and anyone suffering from an illness.

*The publisher would like to thank*
*Steamer Trading Cookshop, Lewes, East Sussex, for the kind loan of props.*